WILDLIFE WATCH

GRAND CANYON ZION & BRYCE

NATIONAL PARKS

By Todd Wilkinson
Photography by Michael H. Francis

NORTHWORD
PRESS, INC
Minocqua, Wisconsin

To Henry Allan and Irene Isabell Carroll Wilkinson,
for showing me nature through the mysteries of the lake

The author extends his sincere gratitude to those with the National Park Service who helped this project along by contributing their time, knowledge and thoughtful review of the text. In particular, special thanks go to Denny Davies, the chief of interpretation at Zion; Edd Franz, Lou Good, and Dan Foster at Bryce Canyon; and L. Greer Price and Anita Davis at Grand Canyon. Finally, a word of praise for the natural history associations in each park (see the section "So You'd Like To Know More?" in the back of this book). Supporting these non-profit institutions goes a long way toward protecting park treasures with the most powerful tool possible: Education.

© Todd Wilkinson, 1995
Photography © Michael H. Francis, 1995
Additional photography © 1995:
    pg. 24—David M. Dennis/Tom Stack and Associates; pg. 70-71—Mike Barlow/Dembinsky Photo Associates; pg. 82—L. Riley/ Bruce Coleman, Inc.; pg. 86—John Gerlach/Dembinsky Photo Associates; pg. 87—John Gerlach/DRK Photo; pg. 94—Tom Bean; pg. 100—Jeff Foott/Bruce Coleman, Inc.—pg. 102-103; M. Kazmers/Dembinsky Photo Associates; pg. 120—Bob and Clara Calhoun/Bruce Coleman, Inc.; pg. 123—Alan G. Nelson/Dembinsky Photo Associates; pg. 136—Stan Osolinski/ Dembinsky Photo Associates; pg. 137—Charles Melton/The Wildlife Collection; pg. 139—Donna Aitkenhead

Cover design by Russell S. Kuepper
Book design by Kenneth A. Hey

NorthWord Press, Inc.
P.O. Box 1360 / Minocqua, WI 54548

For a free catalog describing NorthWord's line of books and gift items call toll free 1-800-336-5666

Printed in Hong Kong

Library of Congress Cataloging-in-Publication Data
Wilkinson, Todd.
        Grand Canyon, Zion, Bryce Canyon/by Todd Wilkinson; photography by Michael H. Francis.
            p. cm.—(A Wildlife watcher's guide)
        Includes bibliographical references.
        ISBN 1-55971-461-1
        1. Zoology—Arizona—Grand Canyon National Park. 2. Zoology—Utah—Zion National Park. 3. Zoology—Utah—Bryce Canyon National Park. 4. Wildlife watching—Arizona—Grand Canyon National Park Guidebooks. 5. Wildlife watching—Utah—Zion National Park—Guidebooks. 6. Wildlife watching—Utah—Bryce Canyon National Park—Guidebooks. 7. Grand Canyon National Park (Ariz.) —Guidebooks. 8. Zion National Park (Utah)—Guidebooks. 9. Bryce Canyon National Park (Utah)—Guidebooks. I. Francis, Michael H. (Michael Harlowe). II. Title. III. Series: Wildlife watcher's guide series.
        QL162.W55 1995
        596.09791'3—dc20   94-41781
                                                                       CIP

Contents

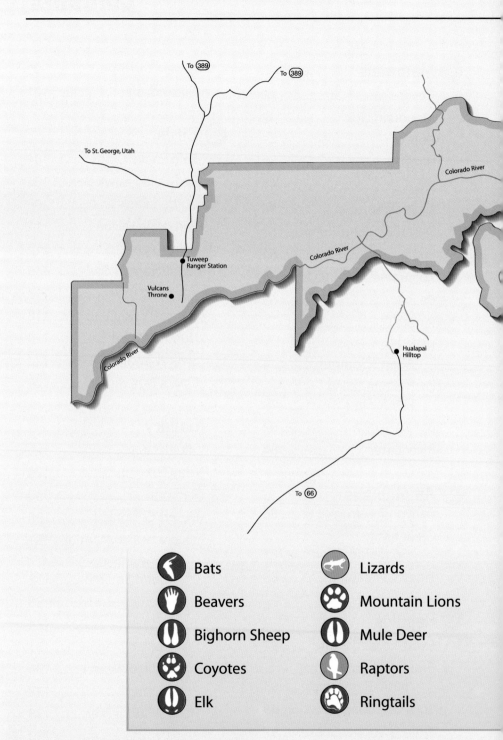

To 389

To 389

To St. George, Utah

Colorado River

Tuweep
Ranger Station

Colorado River

Vulcans
Throne

Colorado River

Hualapai
Hilltop

To 66

	Bats		Lizards
	Beavers		Mountain Lions
	Bighorn Sheep		Mule Deer
	Coyotes		Raptors
	Elk		Ringtails

Grand Canyon National Park

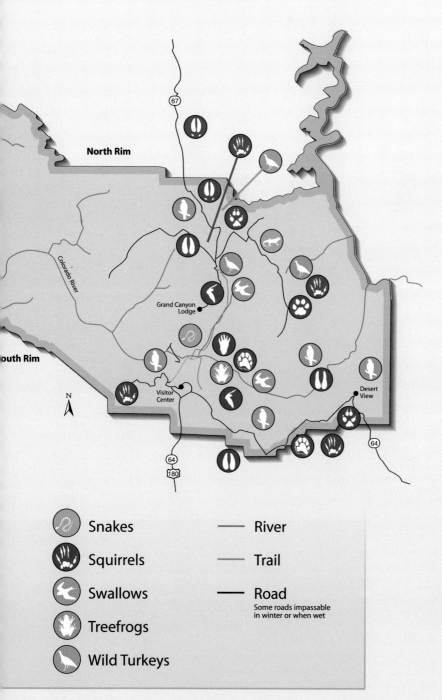

North Rim

67

Colorado River

Grand Canyon Lodge

outh Rim

N

Visitor Center

Desert View

64

64
180

Legend

- 🐍 Snakes
- 🐾 Squirrels
- 🕊 Swallows
- 🐸 Treefrogs
- 🦃 Wild Turkeys

- —— River
- —— Trail
- —— Road
  Some roads impassable in winter or when wet

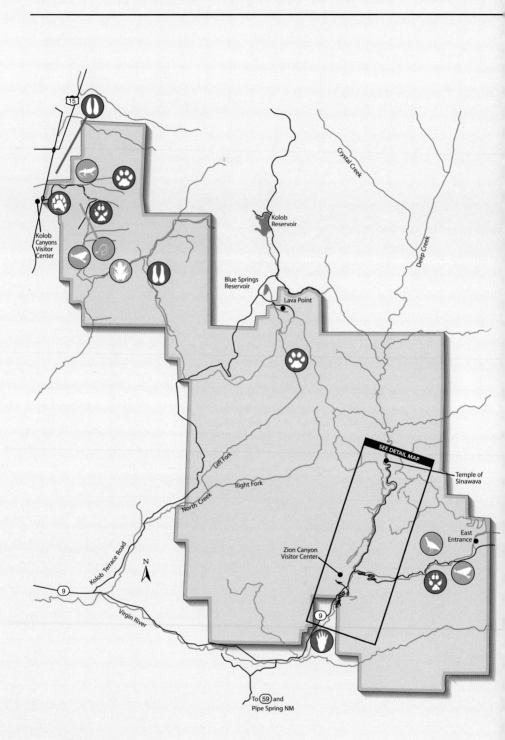

Crystal Creek

Deep Creek

Kolob Reservoir

Blue Springs Reservoir

Lava Point

SEE DETAIL MAP

Temple of Sinawava

Left Fork

Right Fork

North Creek

East Entrance

Kolob Canyons Visitor Center

Zion Canyon Visitor Center

Kolob Terrace Road

Virgin River

N

To 59 and Pipe Spring NM

Zion National Park

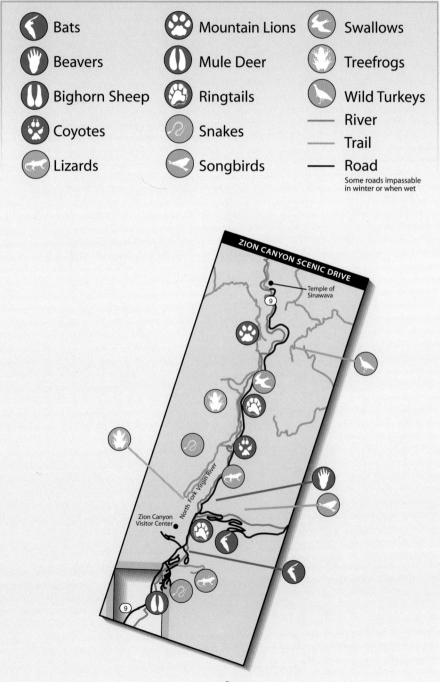

Bats

Beavers

Bighorn Sheep

Coyotes

Lizards

Mountain Lions

Mule Deer

Ringtails

Snakes

Songbirds

Swallows

Treefrogs

Wild Turkeys

River

Trail

Road

Some roads impassable
in winter or when wet

ZION CANYON SCENIC DRIVE

Temple of
Sinawava

9

North Fork Virgin River

Zion Canyon
Visitor Center

9

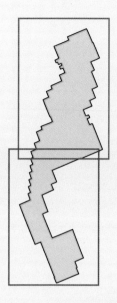

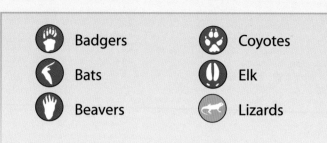

Badgers   Coyotes

Bats   Elk

Beavers   Lizards

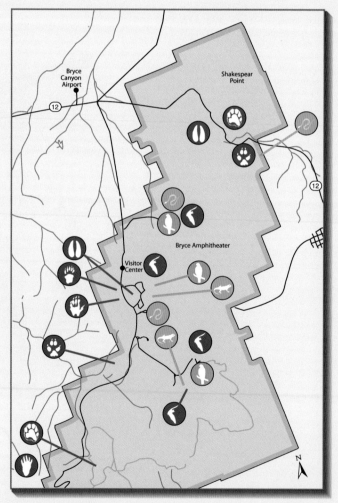

Bryce Canyon National Park

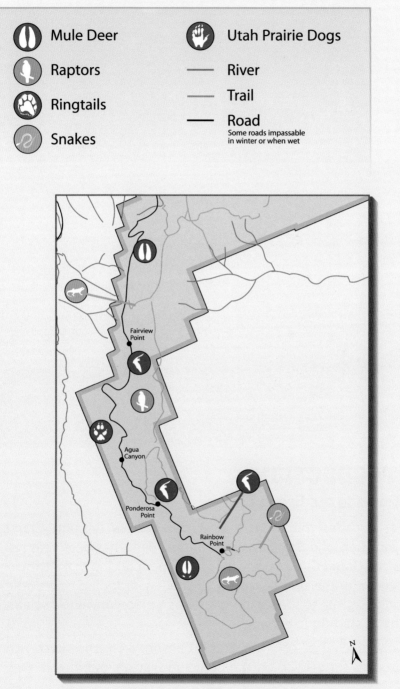

Mule Deer

Raptors

Ringtails

Snakes

Utah Prairie Dogs

—— River

—— Trail

—— Road
Some roads impassable
in winter or when wet

Fairview
Point

Agua
Canyon

Ponderosa
Point

Rainbow
Point

N

INTRODUCTION
Welcome to the Grand Circle

For decades the route that guides visitors through Grand Canyon, Zion, and Bryce Canyon national parks has been referred to as "the Grand Circle." While millions of people who make the circuit come for the slick-rock scenery and jaw-dropping views, little thought is given to the region's status as a place for wildlife safaris. All that is starting to change.

Collectively, not only are Grand Canyon, Zion, and Bryce rich sanctuaries for wildlife on the Colorado Plateau, but in fact, they

reign as one of the best kept secrets in the entire national park system. Indeed, searching for your favorite wildlife species adds a new dimension to any vacation in the national parks.

This book covers a trio of parks that have a long history of human association with the animals that have evolved with the land. We know this because the earliest wildlife watchers thousands of years ago recorded their observations on slabs of stone. Chiseled into the red rock walls are petroglyphic testaments made by native people who celebrated such creatures as the coyote, elk, snake, raven, and lizard. Today, the tradition of documenting flora and fauna continues.

Each year, millions of visitors will peer into the dulcet chasm of the Grand Canyon to see the seventh natural wonder of the world without realizing that along the North Rim one of the most imperiled and stunningly beautiful squirrel species is nearby. Busloads of tour groups will gawk at the vermillion-hued monoliths inside the Bryce Canyon amphitheater without thinking that one of the birds soaring above the cliffs is a peregrine falcon, regarded as one of the great wildlife conservation success stories in North America. And when passing below the sculptured lines of the Checkerboard Mesa in Zion, few grasp that the arroyos and desertscapes which dominate the national park provide habitat for one of the largest populations of mountain lions in the West.

Grand Canyon, Zion, and Bryce are each part of the larger Colorado Plateau, an area covering nearly 130,000 square miles (300,000 square kilometers) across the eroded tableland of Four Corners—Arizona, Utah, New Mexico, and Colorado. Topography holds the parks together and wildlife gives the separate habitats of the region a common affinity.

Some animals will require that you find them by staking out places where they routinely visit, such as water holes and stream courses, forest edges, and sheer drop-offs. To see the furtive animals it may also demand that you learn their habits at certain times of the day (usually first and last sunlight). Other species are there within view but you must train your eye to see them. Often, the easiest way to locate wildlife in the desert Southwest is simply to relax for awhile at a place just off the beaten path and look for movement or listen for sounds coming from nearby vegetation. Often, a whole complement of fascinating creatures is closer than you think.

There are well over 300 species of birds encompassed by the three parks, more than half of which are neotropical flyers—species that spend part of the year in the park and the colder months farther south in the United States, Central and South America. This book obviously cannot cover them all and doesn't attempt to. Rather, this text introduces wildlife watchers to the most popular and the most obvious of the avian inhabitants they might see. For

14

example, it does not mention any members of the Family Emberizidae, that of warblers, blackbirds and orioles which represent the largest grouping of birds in Bryce Canyon; nor does it describe the Tyrant Flycatchers, of which more than a dozen have been seen in Grand Canyon; nor does it describe the array of finches found in Zion. Similarly, this book was not written to cover all the possible reptile and amphibian or rodent species. For more information on the variety of birds, or, for that matter, the range of any other animal found in the parks, write the park individually to request information pertaining to birds, mammals, reptiles, amphibians, and native plants at the addresses listed in the back of this book.

Perhaps no other communities of species are more associated with desert environments than reptiles and amphibians. Hot, rocky, dry environments may appear spartan but after spring rains come they boast biological diversity that is surprisingly fertile. Zion, for example, has over 800 native species of plants, more than anywhere else in Utah, as well as habitat for 75 mammal species, some 270 species of birds and 13 varieties of lizards. Grand Canyon, meanwhile, lists 23 varieties of poisonous and nonpoisonous snakes while Bryce confirms a robust population of avian and mammalian predators.

The purpose of this guide is not to be an encyclopedia of all the possible animals in the parks no matter how common or obscure but rather a collection of wildlife you are most likely to see and where you might go looking to find them. To use this guide, first turn to the section marked "Wildlife Encounters" to find a species you may be interested in, then turn to the table of contents and the park maps. Finally, when planning a route, consider the section "Beginning Your Adventure" which lists a suggested drive in each park that offers the maximum variety of species observed from the roadside.

Visitors from around the world come here to see the scenery—from Europe, Asia, Latin America, and Africa—only to discover that the land is a backdrop to ecosystems teeming with life. Wildlife. We hope this book will lend you a hand in leading you to see nature. It is our intent that it become your passport to some of the premiere wildlife watching in the lower 48 states.

WILDLIFE WATCHER'S CODE OF CONDUCT

Grand Canyon, Zion, and Bryce Canyon are the domains of wildlife. We humans must remember that we are merely guests. As such, visitors assume special responsibilities during their search for park animals and the first goal should be trying to eliminate our impact on the environment, which includes treading lightly on wildlife habitat.

With fewer dollars available to operate national parks, rangers need your helping hand in protecting park resources. One way we can provide assistance is by following a code of conduct that guides our behavior. Here are a few things to consider as you start your park journey.

Never Feed Wildlife

Wild animals in national parks are far better off without human generosity. Throwing any food to wildlife may lead to a harmful dependency, which can make the animals more aggressive and dangerous. In the past, feeding animals has resulted not only in people being bitten or injured but unfortunately it has caused wildlife officials to destroy animals that became trash junkies. Remember, as you decide whether to toss that extra bread crumb to the ground, that instead of being kind you may be handing the animal a death sentence.

Maintain a Safe Viewing Distance

Park regulations strictly forbid humans from leaving their cars and knowingly harassing an animal. If an animal must alter its normal behavior and flee due to your presence, you're too close and should back off. When you invade a wild animal's space, there are a number of things that could happen: (1) You might cause a dangerous encounter with an animal that feels threatened and tries to defend itself. Mother animals with young are particularly sensitive to humans who intrude upon their comfort zone. (2) You may be forcing an animal to flee habitat that is necessary for it to survive. The ethics of appropriate wildlife watching take on even greater meaning during the hot summer and cold winter months when

animals are stressed from lack of available food and water. Spooking them into fleeing may cause them to expend essential fat supplies and jeopardize their survival later on. (3) You may inadvertently be causing resource damage by trampling sensitive plants.

Never advance toward bird nests, because human disturbance of a site encourages abandonment of the nest by parents, and if the nest is located on the ground your trail may lead natural carnivores such as coyotes to the nest site. For a closer view of any species, whether it is a deer or reptile, use a zoom camera lens, a pair of binoculars, or a spotting scope.

Drive Slowly and Cautiously

Those who see the most animals from the roadside in national parks are those who bother to slow down and soak up the scenery. The speed limits in Grand Canyon, Zion, and Bryce Canyon are posted to ensure your safety and the safety of wildlife. Animals may cross the roadway at any moment, but motorists should be particularly alert around dawn and dusk, when many of the larger mammals are most active.

When you do see an animal and decide to stop, find park pullovers (i.e., roadside parking areas) for your safety as well as to minimize traffic congestion and to ensure that you do not drive on delicate plants along the road. It is illegal to park in ditches along all national park roads. To help minimize gridlock, carpool.

Keep a Clean Camp

It goes without saying that litter is the bane of national parks, and all food should be properly stored. Most negative encounters between people and wildlife can be prevented simply by maintaining a clean campsite and storing provisions properly in the trunk of your car where they do not invite bears, ringtails, or insects. While picnicking, remember to keep your food locked in airtight containers that do not allow odors to escape.

If you're camping in the backcountry, hang your food in a tree (or on a provided post) at least 15 feet above the ground and inside a plastic container that cannot be raided by bears or birds. Try to avoid cooking smelly foods that may attract scavengers and never sleep in the same clothes you wore while cooking.

Finally—and this is perhaps the most important part of responsible camping—pack out all trash that you bring into the backcountry. If you're parked in a roadside site, make certain all rubbish is tossed into garbage cans.

Restrain Pets

Pets—particularly barking or unruly dogs—are a liability to wildlife watchers. By their simple presence, pets often frighten the animals that you and others are trying to observe. More alarmingly, pets can cause animals such as bears, mountain lions, and coyotes to exhibit aggressive behavior. Park regulations stipulate that all domestic animals must be under the owner's control and on a leash at all times. Pets are not allowed on nature trails or in the backcountry. If you have a choice, you're advised to leave your pet at home. Besides, it is the humane thing to do. During the summer months, temperatures can reach 120 degrees Fahrenheit (49 degrees Centigrade) which can cause a pet to die of heatstroke. Boarding kennels are available in most of the larger towns outside the parks.

Leave Antlers and Horns Where You Find Them

It is illegal to remove horns and antlers found inside the national parks. They are an important source of nutrients for many smaller mammals, and they serve as poignant reminders of the life and death cycle that continually occurs in wild areas. All three parks provide habitat for horned and antlered animals.

Do Not Use Artificial Calls or Spotlights

Shining an animal at night with your spotlight might give you a better look at a deer or mountain lion but it is strictly illegal in national parks. It is also illegal to summon wildlife with artificial calls or vocal mimmickry.

INTERESTING NOTES

A Call to Wildlife Watchers

Working with limited budgets and shortages of personnel, park rangers recognize that some of the best tools for better understanding the parks are visitors going afield. If you happen to record an unusual animal or bird sighting, the park would like to hear from you by simply filling out a Natural History Observation Card which is available at visitor centers and park entrance stations. The information you provide will help to better protect inhabitants in the parks.

Hantavirus

In 1993, following a very rainy spring and summer, there was an outbreak of a serious disease called Hantavirus that killed several people in the Southwest region of the United States. Scientists believe the outbreak was caused by an explosion in the local population of deer mice which carry and spread the disease through fecal droppings and urine. It has been hypothesized that perhaps Hantavirus has always been present but the abnormal surge of rodent numbers was caused by an abundance of grasses. Alerts have been issued in the parks but no cases have been reported. Still, it is a good idea to avoid areas where deer mice congregate in the backcountry and to keep a clean camp to prevent them from getting into food.

An Ancient Tree

While a pine tree doesn't fall under the category of "wildlife watching," there is an ancient tree species present in Bryce Canyon and nearby Cedar Breaks National Monument that is worth observing considering that it makes the old-growth redwoods in the Pacific Northwest seem like youngsters by comparison. Bristlecone pine (*Pinus longaeva*) can live to be thousands of years old. There is one live trunk in Bryce Canyon thought to be 1,700 years old. It is located near Yovimpa Point along the one mile Bristlecone Loop Trail. Bristlecone pines even older can be found in Cedar Breaks.

The Extirpated: Gone But Not Forgotten

While the Four Corners region speaks to the essence of true wilderness, there are pieces of the aboriginal wildlife puzzle still missing. Gone since earlier in the twentieth century are grizzly bears, gray wolves, and California condors.

Where The Deer and the Antelope Play

Although pronghorn officially are not considered a wildlife component of Bryce Canyon, many of the swift animals are seen along the north end of the park.

Tips For Finding Wildlife

What we really want is a hassle-free way to locate certain species. The most important factors that will influence your watching are the time of year, the habitat, and the time of day. Read each section about the species in which you are interested; then scout the recommended locations. Many animals in these parks are nocturnal (night foraging), or crepuscular (most active at dawn and dusk). As a result, early morning and evening hours when the conditions are cooler are the most productive hours for embarking on visual safaris. At high noon, under the blazing sun, your prospects are poor.

Before you set out, know the tools for safe wildlife watching. Your vehicle is a secure place for observing large mammals. Instead of stepping closer to any animal, consider using a pair of binoculars, a spotting scope, or a long camera lens. Spotting scopes are versatile because they can be carried up a mountain on a trip or mounted to the window of a car. Particularly effective for viewing raptors, spotting scopes are occasionally set up by park rangers at turnouts in order to assist visiting wildlife watchers.

Remember, don't underestimate the value of using your vehicle as a blind. Most large mammals and many bird species have learned to tolerate cars along the roadside as long as visitors stay inside of them.

Photographer Mike Francis recommends that amateur photographers add a 50-300mm zoom camera lens to their equipment bag if possible. A 300mm is a solid lens that allows visitors to get sharp portraits without having to move in too close. The lens most commonly used by professionals is a 400mm. Visitors carrying cameras of any sort (including video cameras) should be advised that the rules of responsible wildlife watching apply equally to them.

Cedar Breaks National Monument

Cedar Breaks National Monument is part of the Grand Circle that often is overlooked by visitors but no park with so little space provides more wildlife watching opportunities. This part of the National Park System receives administrative support from Zion but geologically it is identical to Bryce Canyon. Pink spires and natural chimney columns tower from majestic canyon walls. Located nearly two miles above sea level, temperatures at the monument during summer and autumn days often are 20 degrees cooler than in the other parks, which makes it a welcome retreat. In fact, some of the plant species found here have a kindredness with flora that can exist only on the tundra. In the short span of only five miles, visitors have potential opportunities of seeing elk, mule deer, coyotes, long-tailed weasels, mountain lions, black bears, yellow-bellied marmots, red-tailed hawks, golden eagles, Clark's nutcrackers, and a variety of neo-tropical songbirds. It also is home to some of the oldest trees in North America, the Bristlecone pine, and is rich in wildflowers.

Highway 143 which runs through the northeast corner of the park is open year-round while Highway 148 is closed to traffic in the winter. Cedar Breaks is situated 22 miles from Cedar City, Utah, just off United States Interstate 15. For more information, write: Superintendent, Cedar Breaks National Monument, P.O. Box 749, Cedar City, UT 84720.

THE POISONOUS ONES

No narrative about wildlife watching in desert parks would be complete without first mentioning what's on everybody's mind—the creeping and crawling animals, the poisonous ones that make us squirm. For the record, there are at least a half dozen different species of rattlesnakes which fall under the reptilian

Giant Hairy Scorpion

family *Crotalus*—more colloquially known as poisonous pit vipers—that emit venom from glands located near the fangs. Some of these serpents are discussed later in the book, along with the infamous banded gila monster, but for now turn your attention to the others—the scorpions, spiders, ants and centipedes—which potentially are deadly, particularly for those whose bodies are ill-equipped to deal with foreign proteins.

It may provide comfort to wildlife watchers knowing that few poisonous critters are interested in encountering humans and would like nothing better than to be left alone. Sometimes, however, we might bump into them by accident. The majority of bites from scorpions, spiders, and rattlesnakes occur because a hand was put where it shouldn't have been. It is not wise to hastily grab a log for the campfire or pick up a rock without first carefully looking to see what's beneath it. Use care and caution.

There are, according to some estimates, a minimum of 20 scorpion species that are found in Arizona alone and one of the deadliest, a tiny creature called the sculptured scorpion (*Centruroides sculpturatus*) is found not only in the Sonoran Desert along the border between the United States and Mexico but in the bottom of the Grand Canyon. Scorpions resemble lobsters, with arm pincers at the front of their body and a looping tail at the posterior. They are highly defensive creatures that strike when they feel attacked or provoked. Like all scorpions, the sculptured scorpion injects its venom with a stinger located at the end of its tail. It is the most poisonous of its kind in the United States, can be identified by its yellow, slender tail. Its venom is neurotoxic which means it affects the central nervous system. Some 70 species of scorpions occur in the United States but rest assured that most do not represent a mortal threat to humans.

Being night hunters, scorpions are inactive during the day and seek shelter in piles of brush or beneath rocks or even in drawers or closets. At night when they explore, they may also crawl into beds or clothing or shoes which is why you should check your sheets before retiring, and shake out your sneakers or pants in the morning if you've been camping outside, particularly in the bottom of the canyon.

If you suffer a scorpion sting, which can be prevented rather simply by sleeping on a cot at night, watching where you reach and not walking barefoot, contact a physician as soon as possible. Don't panic. The odds are remote that your sting was inflicted by a sculptured scorpion, which means the wound probably will only have an effect in the local area where it was rendered.

The same rules of caution apply for black widow spiders (*Latrodectus mactans*) and brown recluse spiders (*Loxosceles reclusa*). Black widows, of course, are known for eating their male partners after mating. The spider is recognized by its large round abdomen that has a bright red pattern underneath which looks like an hour glass. Outside, black widows can be found in leafy desert floors and sandy soil. The venom from a black widow is considered highly toxic and demands medical treatment at once. Perhaps the place where black widows might pose the greatest risk is in outhouses. The spider hides under the toilet seat waiting for insects and when someone sits down, it may bite in self defense. Look beneath the seat before you sit.

The interesting aspect about human fear relating to black widows is the fact that the spiders are found throughout the southern United States but most people think of them only as desert species, which means that if you have not encountered one already it is not likely that you will encounter one now if you take the proper precautions. This same rationale holds true with brown recluse spiders. They tend to gather in dark areas of a house, beneath porches, in bookshelves and camping gear if it is left undisturbed for a length of time. They have an orange-yellow head with a distinct dark brown marking that looks like a fiddle or bass. Again, they are found in any state.

The final venomous creature is the centipede, an arthropod with many legs. There are hundreds of centipede species in the United States and most inject venom through claws found under their head. Some of the largest species occur in the Southwest, with one species being a foot long. The color on them ranges from dull olive brown to red or orange. Although the venom is lethal only to those who have allergic reactions, a pinch is known to hurt nonetheless.

HABITATS

Wildlife do not congregate in certain areas of the parks by happenstance. You will see them in an area because that's where they eat, find cover from predators, nest, rest, burrow, or breed. The following is a quick primer on the kinds of habitat you will encounter in the three parks and the animals associated with each.

Sagebrush: The plateau and rim shrublands around the Grand Canyon, on the eastern side of Zion, and the northern edge of Bryce Canyon. Typically, it is found from 5,000 feet to 6,500 feet (1,500-2,000 meters) and marks the entrance to the pinyon-juniper-oak forest. The species that one can expect to find here are mule deer, ground squirrels, coyote, badger, bobcat, rabbits, long-tailed weasel, turkey vultures, ravens, pronghorn, snakes, and raptors such as red-tailed hawks. In the Grand Canyon this includes areas leading to the North and South rims. In Zion this includes meadows outside the east and south entrances. In Bryce this includes areas at the north end of the park.

Pinyon-Juniper-Oak: Forest habitat of pinyon pine, Utah juniper, Gambel oak and shrub oak at elevations between 4,000 and 7,000 feet (1,200 to 2,100 meters). It is found in all three parks. Species one can expect to find here are mule deer, coyote, black bear, mountain lion, wild turkey, squirrels, chipmunks, owls and possibly foxes, packrats, bighorns, goshawks, common raven, owls, rabbits, ringtail, jays, hummingbirds. In the Grand Canyon it includes south Rim and Coconino Plateau. In Zion it includes Zion Canyon in the vicinity of Zion Lodge, and Kolob Canyon Road. In Bryce it includes the area around the main visitor center and rim of the amphitheater, also below the rim parkwide.

Coniferous Forest: Ponderosa pine with Douglas-fir, white fir (i.e. needle-bearing trees) as well as aspen, Gambel oak, and subalpine mixed conifers of Engelmann spruce and subalpine fir above 7,000 feet (2,100 meters). The species that one can expect to find are mule deer, coyote, black bear, mountain lion, wild turkey, Kaibab

27

and other squirrels, owls and goshawks, woodpeckers, grouse, ground squirrels, elk, bobcat. In the Grand Canyon it includes the North Rim and the South Rim ponderosa habitats. In Zion it includes Horse Pasture Plateau, the upper end of Zion Canyon, and the east entrance areas. In Bryce it includes the area from Whiteman Bench to Rainbow Point and points overlooking the amphitheater.

Riparian: Streamside corridors with water-dependent trees such as cottonwood, salt cedar, and willow. This generally is the richest habitat for wildlife watching. Species one can expect to find are bald eagle, mule deer, coyote, mountain lion, desert bighorn sheep, snakes, rodents, skunks, beaver, otter, black bear, lizards, frogs, songbirds, raptors. In the Grand Canyon, riparian areas are found along the Colorado River and its descending tributaries. In Zion it's along the Virgin River. In Bryce it's along Water Canyon, Rigg's Spring, Sheep Creek, Swamp Canyon, and Yellow Creek.

Creosotebush: Includes vegetation such as Mohave desertscrub below 2,000 feet (600 meters) in elevation and dominated by creosotebush, white bursage, ocotillo, brittlebush, barrel cactus and other cacti. The species one can expect to find here are snakes and lizards, raptors, roadrunners, ground squirrels, coyote, mountain lion, bobcat, Gambel's quail, badger, rabbits. In the Grand Canyon it is found in the western end. In Zion it includes the south park entrance near Springdale. Bryce does not have this habitat.

Blackbrush: Classic desertscrub habitat comprised of blackbrush, yucca, Utah agave, and catclaw acacia. Similar species are found here as in Creosotebush, including mule deer. In the Grand Canyon, it includes the Tonto Platform of about 3500 feet (1100 meters). In Zion it includes areas around the southern entrance and northwest entrance at Kolob.

Grassland: Open expanse that may have sagebrush on the lower fringes. In the Grand Canyon, it includes areas as diverse as the desert grassland type as found in Toroweap Valley at 4,600 feet (1,400 meters) and the mountain grasslands of the Kaibab Plateau 9,000 feet (2,700 meters). The species one can expect to find here

are mule deer, raptors, Utah prairie dogs, badger, rodents, coyote, gray fox. In Bryce this habitat is located near the visitor center.

Mountain Scrub: Transitional zone that includes both chaparral and deciduous shrublands from 4,000 to 7,000 feet (1,200 to 2,100 meters). The plants here include manzanita, silk-tassel brush, New Mexico locust, shrub live oak, serviceberry. The species one can expect to find here include mule deer, elk, fox, bobcat, mountain lion, rodents, raptors. In the Grand Canyon such habitat is evident on both the North and South rims. In Zion it exists in the entry ways to the park and some parts of the interior. In Bryce this includes most forested areas of the park.

SUGGESTED DRIVES

The three parks are located within a few hours of one another. Most people set aside a week to visit them all.

Grand Canyon (Northern Arizona)

There are three primary entrances to the Grand Canyon. The north entrance is accessible via highway 67 between Jacob Lake and the North Rim. The south entrance is located along U.S. Highway 180 between Valle, Arizona (north of Williams and Flagstaff) and Grand Canyon Village. The southeast entrance is located along Highway 64 west of Cameron. The south and east entrances are connected by an interior park road called the East Rim Drive. The main park visitor center is located at Grand Canyon Village. Note: The North Rim is closed in winter.

Logistics here will determine your route. The more developed and crowded South Rim of the Grand Canyon requires a 215-mile, five-hour drive from the North Rim. The South Rim is the preferred and easier destination for visitors coming from the south via Phoenix, Flagstaff, Las Vegas, or Los Angeles, but while it shares the canyon it is a different world from the other side. The North Rim is higher, cooler, and quieter and is more easily accessible to people coming from the north and cities like Salt Lake City and Denver. Nonetheless, wildlife watching from either vantage, not to forget, of course, hikes or floats into the maw of the canyon itself, is excellent particularly for early risers and those who plan in advance. Habitat for desert and subalpine forest creatures abounds in the Grand Canyon which stretches for almost 280 miles.

On the South Rim: Grand Canyon Village is located 60 miles north of Williams, Arizona, by way of route 64 and Interstate 40, and 80 miles north of Flagstaff via route 180. Start your safari on the South Rim by first stopping at the main park visitor center in Grand Canyon Village and asking ranger-naturalists about wildlife watching opportunities. They will have the latest reports about birds, mammals, and reptiles. Then set out along the 26-mile East Rim Drive to Desert View, making stops at both Grandview and Moran points to survey the canyon below for birds. Along the South Rim is the pinyon-juniper forest, which offers home to scrub and pinyon jays, desert cottontails, gray fly-catchers, and a raven or turkey vulture. There might be a horned lizard on the rocks along the way. Continue east past the Tusayan Ruins, offering a glimpse of Pueblo Indian life 800 years ago, and on to the East Entrance.

Another popular route is the eight-mile West Rim Drive to Hermit's Rest which is closed to private vehicles from Memorial Day to the end of September. A shuttle bus is available to take you there from the parking lot. It is well worth the effort of exploring and a good place for birding, particularly watching raptors soar over the canyon. For those who want to stretch their legs, there is also a hiking trail that follows the rim from Yavapai Point to Hermit's Rest. Should you decide to drive to the North Rim or Zion from here, there is a little-known state park along the way that provides excellent opportunities for seeing bison. The House Rock Buffalo Ranch is 20 miles south of Highway 89A on Forest Road 445.

On the North Rim: It is a 45-mile drive from Jacob Lake to the North Rim of the Grand Canyon along North Rim Parkway (Highway 67). This drive is closed during the winter but offers excellent wildlife viewing from mid-May to mid-October. Along the way is the Kaibab National Forest, which sits across the Kaibab Plateau. The plateau was the subject decades ago of a controversy involving mule deer when the federal government moved to kill all of the deer's predators. Although the deer population dramatically increased, the animals overate the available vegetation and the population severely diminished. Today, the area still is known for its mule deer hunting but wildlife officials now take a kinder view toward predators. At the north entrance, there is the possibility of seeing elk, mule deer, red-tailed hawks, wild turkeys, and ravens during the spring and autumn.

The Cape Royal Road is 23 miles long and offers an exceptional view of the canyon as well as excellent opportunities for seeing deer, wild turkeys, Kaibab squirrels, possibly even coyotes and mountain lions if you get an early start. The canyon overlook is also an excellent place for spying raptors. Another good avenue for finding animals is the road to Point Imperial where blue grouse and Kaibab squirrels are common.

If you have time and don't want to hike, you can ride a mule into the canyon by registering at the Grand Canyon Lodge. During the day, use your binoculars to look for soaring raptors—hawks, eagles, falcons, and vultures—and picnic at one of the established turnouts. But don't feed the members of the crow family—jays, ravens, nutcrackers—that may join you along with golden-mantled ground squirrels.

Along the rim at dusk, look for white-throated swifts and green swallows joining bats in scavenging insects. The campgrounds along the rim attract a variety of hummingbirds and the rocks are promontories for horned lizards. It is not uncommon for bobcats, or at least their tracks, to be spotted along the hiking trails.

Zion (Southern Utah)

There are three entrances to Zion. The first is the East Entrance Road along Highway 9, also called the Zion-Mt. Carmel Highway, which leads both to the Zion Canyon Scenic Drive and the south entrance at Springdale, Utah. The south entrance is home of the park's main visitor center. The third entrance is located just off Interstate U.S. 15 at Exit 40 (south of Cedar City) and leads to Kolob Canyon Road and a viewpoint at the end of the road. This entrance is where the Kolob Canyons Visitor Center is located.

The best wildlife watching in Zion occurs off the highway in the backcountry. For people with limited time, the main route between the south entrance at Springdale, where the Zion Canyon Visitor Center is located, and the east entrance along the Zion-Mt. Carmel Highway is a good compromise because there are plenty of places along the way to hike. Make sure, however,

33

that you make a sidetrip in your car up the Zion Canyon Scenic Drive, a dead-end route that leads to Temple of Sinawava and shadows the North Fork of the Virgin River. This section, especially, is fruitful because the available trails offer possibilities for seeing a wide variety of birds, mammals, reptiles and amphibians.

Wildlife need water. Without it, the diversity of desert parks would literally dry up. While Zion has many washes that run seasonally or even daily following sudden thundershowers, there are a few permanent water holes and streams that attract a convergence of species. Those areas are the Virgin River and its related tributaries, Kolob and Blue Springs Reservoirs, and Springdale Ponds. The Virgin is the park's wildlife centerpiece.

Bryce Canyon (Southern Utah)

There is one primary entrance to Bryce Canyon and a second stretch of Highway 12 which runs through the Tropic Canyon between U.S. 89 and the town of Tropic. The main entrance is located off of Highway 12 (east of Panguitch, Utah) and is a dead-end route through the center of the park. The visitor center is located along this route.

Bryce Canyon National Park has 35 miles (roughly 56 kilometers) of paved roadway that lead to scenic overlooks and along the way some pretty fine opportunities for seeing a range of wildlife. The main route is a dead end that stops at the southern end of the park at Rainbow Point. Flanking the roadway from roughly Whiteman Bench to Rainbow Point are Bryce's famous Pink Cliffs and a chasm that is backdropped by extraordinary geological wonders. Again, this is merely a backdrop, for along the road in the Ponderosa pine forest, it is possible by venturing out at sunrise and sunset to see mule deer, great horned owls, goshawks, coyotes, and even more secretive predators like black bears and mountain lions.

The centerpiece of Bryce Canyon is the amphitheater and into this drop-off you are certain to see an array of raptors: red-tailed hawks, peregrine falcons, American kestrels, perhaps a golden eagle and maybe a turkey vulture circling in the sky.

More than 164 species of birds either breed or pass through the park annually. At dusk, with the setting sun, you also will see the emergence of bats as well as swifts and swallows gobbling insects. Of course, the best wildlife watching is awaiting those who stop their cars and set out on a hike with a good field guide and plenty of water in their pack. The backcountry holds promise for seeing coyotes and mountain lions as they follow mule deer to lower elevations in the autumn and winter.

WILDLIFE ENCOUNTERS

Here's a chart to help you estimate your chance of observing these species in Grand Canyon, Zion, and Bryce Canyon.

■ Common   On any given day, you stand a good chance of encountering one or more of this species.

▨ Irregular   By simply driving through the park without any information, you may see these species on chance encounters. However, by using the tips in this book, you improve your chances of seeing the animal.

□ Rare   While these animals have been seen in the park, they are spotted so rarely that it is impossible to predict whether you'll encounter the species.

— None   Species not found in the park.

MAMMALS

	Grand Canyon	Zion	Bryce		Grand Canyon	Zion	Bryce
Badger	▨	▨	▨	Mule Deer	■	■	■
Bat				Porcupine	■	▨	■
Big Brown Bat	■	■	■	Pronghorn	□	□	■
California Myotis	■	▨	▨	Ringtail	▨	▨	▨
Long-legged Myotis	▨	■	■	Skunk			
Pallid Bat	■	■	▨	Spotted Skunk	■	■	■
Silver-haired Bat	■	□	■	Striped Skunk	■	■	■
Western Pipistrelle	■	■	▨	Squirrel			
Western Small-footed Myotis	■	■	■	Abert's Squirrel	■	—	—
Yuma Myotis	▨	■	▨	Golden-mantled Ground Squirrel	■	□	■
Beaver	▨	▨	▨	Kaibab Squirrel	■	—	—
Black Bear	□	□	□	Red Squirrel	■	■	■
Bobcat	□	□	□	Rock Squirrel	■	■	■
Chipmunk				White-tailed Antelope Squirrel	■	■	□
Cliff Chipmunk	■	■	▨	Utah Prairie Dog	—	—	■
Least Chipmunk	■	■	■	Rabbit			
Uinta Chipmunk	■	■	■	Black-tailed Jack Rabbit	▨	■	▨
Coyote	▨	▨	▨	Desert Cottontail	■	▨	▨
Desert Bighorn Sheep	▨	□	□	Nuttail's Cottontail	▨	▨	▨
Elk	▨	□	▨	River Otter	□	□	□
Gray Fox	▨	▨	▨	Raccoon	□	□	□
Long-tailed Weasel	▨	▨	▨	Yellow-bellied Marmot	□	▨	▨
Mountain Lion	□	□	□				

BIRDS

	Grand Canyon	Zion	Bryce
American Kestrel	■	■	■
Bald Eagle	■	☑	■
Black-billed Magpie	☑	☑	■
Bluebird	■	■	■
Blue Grouse	■	■	■
Chickadee	■	■	■
Clark's Nutcracker	■	☑	■
Common Raven	■	■	■
Cooper's Hawk	☑	☑	☑
Gambel's Quail	☑	☑	☑
Golden Eagle	☑	☑	☑
Goshawk	■	☑	■
Woodpecker	■	■	■
Hummingbird			
Black-chinned	■	■	■

	Grand Canyon	Zion	Bryce
Broad-tailed	■	■	■
Costa's	■	■	☑
Jay			
Pinyon Jay	■	■	■
Scrub Jay	■	■	■
Steller's Jay	■	■	■
Nuthatch	■	■	■
Peregrine Falcon	☑	☑	☑
Red-tailed Hawk	■	■	■
Road Runner	☑	☑	□
Turkey Vulture	■	■	■
White-throated Swift	■	■	■
Wild Turkey	■	☑	☑
Violet-green Swallow	■	■	■

REPTILES/ AMPHIBIANS

	Grand Canyon	Zion	Bryce
Collared Lizard	■	■	☑
Desert Striped Whipsnake	■	■	■
Desert Tortoise	□	□	□
Gila Monster	□	□	□
Gopher Snake	■	■	■
Grand Canyon Rattlesnake	☑	—	—
Great Basin (Western) Rattlesnake	☑	■	■
Northern Sagebrush/ Side Blotched Lizards	■	■	■
Plateau Lizard	■	■	☑
Short-horned Lizard	■	■	■
Whiptail Lizard	■	■	☑
Yellowback Spiny Lizard	■	■	☑

OTHER

	Grand Canyon	Zion	Bryce
Black Widow Spider	☑	☑	☑
Centipede	☑	☑	☑
Recluse Spider	☑	☑	☑
Scorpion	☑	☑	☑
Tarantula	□	□	□

37

MAMMALS

COYOTE

The coyote (*Canis latrans*) deserves its place as an icon of the Southwest. There is something primordial and enchanting about singing coyotes interrupting the blackness of night with yipping melodies. Native peoples celebrate these wild dogs in oral legends and pictures carved into stone. It does not matter where one hikes in the desert because, whether in view, or by pawprint or bark, the "singing trickster" is nearby.

In the absence of wolves, which were extirpated by federal bounty hunters decades ago, coyotes have emerged at the top of the canid food chain. Instead of vanishing as their canid brethren did, coyotes have proven themselves to be indomitable survivors, adapting to the human suburbs of Phoenix or Las Vegas or Salt Lake City as easily as they delineate their territories in the wilderness of national parks.

Grand Canyon, Zion, and Bryce Canyon offer different types of habitat but coyotes thrive in each park because of their versatility. To give an idea of how common coyotes are, Grand Canyon park officials say that coyotes find a niche in all seven of the park's terrestrial habitat types.

Wildlife watchers routinely confuse coyotes with wolves. Since there currently are no wolves in the three national parks cited in this book, identification of coyotes becomes easier and there should be little trouble mistaking coyotes for their smaller canid cousin, the fox.

Coyotes resemble mid-sized dogs; they weigh around 20 to 30 pounds, sometimes more, and have fluffy tails that point downward as the animal trots along. In spring and summer, their coat is brownish-red, though it turns gray as winter snows advance. The undersides of coyotes are usually white, regardless of the season. Their long snouts and perked ears are defining features of the face.

Whether you're backpacking at a distant campsite or parked in a developed roadside campground, physical clues will let you know if a coyote has been using the area. The first indication is scat (feces), which is tubular like a dog's, often with pieces of hair or bone fragments from the animal's last meal—rabbits, rodents, grasshoppers, carrion from deer, elk, bighorn sheep, possibly the eggs deposited by ground nesting birds or their young, and sometimes even plants. Another indicator of coyote presence is their tracks, which look like a dog's but measure at least 2 1/2 inches long and are highlighted by four toe and claw imprints.

Earlier in this century, federal wildlife officials tried to eradicate coyotes from many parts of the West because they thought these predators posed a threat to game animals as well as livestock. They still are trapped today but within the parks they are afforded refuge.

Though normally nocturnal, coyotes may be seen in the park at any hour of the day. They will be most active, however, around dawn and dusk. In spring, roughly two months after breeding, coyote females dig dens and give birth to between five and seven pups. Some coyote pairs stay together for years; the male hunts for the female as she nurses the young. The average life-span of a coyote is about ten years.

Where To Find Coyotes

Grand Canyon: Coyotes are seen along the North Rim on the Tonto Platform, below the South Rim, and on the rim itself.

Zion: Coyotes routinely are seen in the creosotebush and blackbrush country and also in the canyons.

Bryce Canyon: Although uncommon, coyotes have been seen at East Creek Meadows.

MOUNTAIN LION

Mountain lions possess a certain mystique that transcends their reputation of being furtive and truly effective prowlers. For one thing, they are the largest wildcat found in North America. For another, they're known by different names in different parts of the country. Some of the monikers include cougar, puma, and catamount but it is perhaps the scientific name (*Felis concolor*) which means "cat of one color" that physically describes these prowlers most aptly. It would be extremely difficult to mistake these tawny-colored cats, provided, of course, that you come across one, which is a rare event indeed.

Biologists estimate that about 16,000 mountain lions inhabit the lower 48 states, though that number appears to be increasing. The Four Corners region (that is, the place where the states of Utah, Colorado, New Mexico, and Arizona converge) offers exceptional habitat for mountain lions; some of the premier range for them, in fact, in the whole country. Extremely remote, rural, and rugged, the landscape affords plenty of terrain for cats to hunt without being persecuted by its chief enemy—humans.

Weighing between 75 and 200 pounds at adulthood, mountain lions are equipped with long, retractable claws, enabling them to

climb trees as easily as they scale precipitously steep slopes and arroyo walls. Agile and fleet, mature lions can leap nearly 20 feet in a single bound, and their favorite hunting method involves waiting in ambush and then pouncing upon prey.

Mule deer are the main staple of their diet in all three parks, but lions also prey upon elk, desert sheep, porcupine, beaver, ground foraging birds, and rabbits. Studies show that the average adult female and her young can subsist on roughly one mule deer per week.

Over the course of its nightly hunting sojourn, a mountain lion may travel a dozen or more miles, typically along river drainages where its prey are found. The hours near sunrise and sunset are the best times for cat watching, though any sighting likely is accidental since cats are aware of your presence usually long before you become aware of theirs.

Although mountain lions rarely approach park visitors,

humans have good reason to respect these animals, as several people have been injured or killed in cat encounters over the past decade. And in most cases, the attack was prompted by hungry cats mistaking people for prey. Biologists and wildlife investigators suspect that many human/cat encounters involve sub-adult animals that are trying to establish their own territories and have not yet mastered the skills of catching mule deer. The recommended response for people who are confronted with a curious lion is similar to what's recommended for encountering black bears. Never run from a lion should you meet one in a campground or on a trail. Running triggers the predator instinct in the lion, and the animal likely will chase. Instead, act as aggressively as possible by shouting in an assertive tone and waving your arms to make yourself appear as big as possible. Do not crouch or "play dead." If yelling fails to drive the lion away, consider using rocks or sticks to impede its advance.

Signs of mountain lion presence include copious scat ranging from dark spheres to pellets, often containing traces of whatever the lion ingested. Traces of hair or bones are common. Tracks, measuring between three and four inches in diameter, are wider than they are long. The imprint of four toes makes the prints resemble those of a housecat.

Breeding takes place in late winter or early spring, and a litter of one to six kittens is delivered in early summer. Young lions leave their mothers one to two years after birth and adults maintain a solitary existence except during mating. Mountain lions maintain a den, but they do not sleep during the winter as bears do. Active all year, the size of their population corresponds to the availability of prey.

At one time earlier in this century, cougars were aggressively killed by federal bounty hunters because they were perceived as a threat to domestic livestock herds and wildlife, particularly game species. But modern thinking acknowledges their important role in the health of ecosystems.

Unfortunately, wildlife officials speculate that as human development continues to encroach upon lion habitat, encounters will continue to occur.

Where To Find Mountain Lions

Remember that people should never approach a lion, no matter how docile the animal behaves. In addition, pet owners should make sure their animals are under control if a mountain lion enters a campground because pets have been known to attract lions.

Grand Canyon: Mountain lions try to avoid people and there have been far more sightings of lions on the North Rim than on the South Rim. After a rain, lion tracks sometimes can be found on trails both on top of the rim and below it.

Zion: During the autumn, winter and spring, cats have been seen along the North Fork of the Virgin River up Zion Canyon as well as in the vicinity of Kolob Canyons Road near the Middle Fork of Taylor Creek in the northwest section of the park. They normally are hunting mule deer.

Bryce Canyon: Mountain lion tracks, scat, and kills are sometimes found along the canyon overlooks and below. Park biologists say between 5 and 12 mountain lions inhabit the Bryce environs. Sightings have taken place year-round in all locations. In 1993, for example, a lioness and her cub were seen in the vicinity of the Visitor Center.

BOBCAT

Grand Canyon, Zion, and Bryce Canyon lie in the heart of bobcat range. Bobcats (*Felis rufus*) are the most widely distributed wildcat that is indigenous to the North American continent. As many as 1.5 million bobcats are believed to inhabit the United States. These predators, which bear a striking resemblance to the average tabby housecat (but larger), take their name from their classic stubby tails.

Bobcats are similar in appearance to lynx, but lynx are not found this far south. Bobcats weigh between 20 and 60 pounds but they are capable of preying on animals such as young mule deer equal to their own weight. You can identify a bobcat by the brownish spots on its coat, by the black tufts of hair that extend from the top of its ears, and by the knobby or "bobbed" tail which is never more than five inches long. The coat turns gray during winter. Even when the animal isn't actually in view you may encounter signs that a bobcat has been using the area. Its tracks and scat resemble those of a coyote.

Although they are quite adept at climbing trees, they only scale trees as a last-resort means of escape. Instead, they prefer combing the open scrub brush and desert topography in search of rabbits, young deer, wildfowl, rodents, and even reptiles. During the day, bobcats lay low, often resting in a secure spot in the rocks; at night, they wander over many miles at a time.

Breeding takes place in late winter to early spring, and a litter of one to seven kittens (usually two or three) is delivered in May. Despite the fact that fur trapping is allowed just outside the border of parks, bobcat numbers appear to be stable.

Where To Find Bobcats

Like mountain lions, bobcats range across all three parks. However, they are equally secretive and as wary of humans as their larger feline cousins. As a result, it is virtually impossible to predict when and where these cats will be seen.

BLACK BEAR

Two words summarize the place of black bears in the hearts of visitors to the national parks: The words are *Ursus americanus*, which is the Latin scientific description of "American bear." Black bears exist in all three parks though they tend to maintain a low profile. Only those marauders which become habituated to human food and raid garbage cans make the news.

Black bears are the largest wild omnivores (meat and plant eaters) in the region and the most widely distributed ursine on the North American continent. Here, they occupy a niche that stretches from mountain forests to river corridors that slice through the desert. It's a mistake, however, to assume black bears come in only one color. Besides their stereotypical coal-black coats, black bears, depending on their parents, may appear with pelage that is blonde, chocolate, cinnamon, or reddish brown. Visitors frequently mistake lighter-colored black bears for grizzly bears, their larger cousins. Grizzlies, however, have been absent from the Southwest for decades.

The extirpation of grizzlies, done at the behest of ranchers, has only heightened public awareness and respect for black bears. Physical characteristics that aid in identification are white markings that appear on the bellies of some animals and tan-colored muzzles. Adult boars (males) weigh between 200 and 400 pounds; sows weigh 150 to 300 pounds.

The wildlife watcher may find signs indicating that black bears are in the vicinity. The clues will be found in the mud or sand, probably along a river bottom or near a water hole. The most obvious indicators are tracks. Black bears walk "plantigrade," which, like humans, means that they stroll flat footed and leave behind human-like footprints. The impression of five toes usually is visible, but the pawprint is wider than a human's footprint, and it usually contains claw marks in front of the toes. The tracks also are no more than seven inches long.

Another sure hint of bear presence is scat. Bear scat may be tubular and dark colored, and it reflects the animal's diet.

When bears are feeding on carrion, for example, the scat is firm and sometimes laden with bones or fur. The texture is diarrhetic (runny), however, when the animal is nourished on a diet of berries later in the summer. Then the droppings may appear in piles.

Black bears are opportunistic scavengers that are not fussy about what they eat. They may grub for insects, small rodents, grasses, plant roots, berries, fish, or meat from dead animals. It is essential that park visitors maintain a clean camp at all times and refrain from feeding bears, because habituation can lead to human injury and the destruction or removal of bears from the ecosystem. Feeding bears is illegal and punishable by a fine.

Contrary to popular notion, black bears do not hibernate; rather, they retreat to their winter dens and slumber in a state of dormancy with reduced blood flow and a slowed metabolism, relying upon stored body fat for nourishment. They can and do awaken periodically during the winter months, especially during warm spells.

Nature has provided black bears with a unique means of reproducing. Although sows and boars breed in early summer, development of the embryo is delayed until autumn, when the expectant mother enters her den. During her slumber, beginning in late November or so, between one and four (but usually two) fetuses grow in the mother's womb. Cubs are born toward the end of winter; they survive in the den from an initial birthweight of about 12 ounces to more than 10 pounds by the time they see their first daylight in April. Cubs usually remain with their mother until their second summer, then begin to forage and den on their own.

Not only are black bears good swimmers, but they are highly skilled at climbing trees. Sharp claws enable them to scale thin ponderosa pine. Mothers are hyper-protective of their young and will not hesitate to protect the babies against intruders. A well-known rule of the backcountry is to make noise as you hike on the trail to let black bears know you are approaching.

Of course, it never is wise to approach a black bear, no matter how inviting the animal seems. Bears are wild and dangerous. If you are away from the roadside and unable to get inside your car, stand your ground and make noise in an effort to scare the animal away. Try not to look the bear in the eyes. If the bear continues to approach, fight the animal off; and if that doesn't work, lie in the fetal position with your arms covering your face and neck.

Black bears are hunted outside the park boundaries and in some areas poachers have targeted bears for their gall bladders, claws, and trophy heads. Citizens can play a major role in helping to protect bears by reporting suspicious activity to park rangers.

Where To Find Black Bears

National Park Service regulations strictly prohibit visitors from encroaching within 100 yards (300 feet) of bears. If you feel the need to get close to black bears, use a telephoto lens, spotting scope or binoculars.

Grand Canyon: Few black bears have been sighted inside the

canyon itself. The majority of sightings have taken place on both rims.

Bryce Canyon: The park has a small migratory population of black bears which converge inside the park in late summer and early autumn to eat ripening current and other berries.

ELK

Elk (*Cervus elaphus*) are the largest members of the deer family found within the Colorado Plateau. While their large size and physical markings make them easy to recognize, elk are somewhat elusive. You will need patience finding them.

The best times for seeing elk are spring and autumn, when the animals are migrating between the high meadows where they spend the summer grazing on grasses, and the lower-elevation winter ranges that are not buried in deep snow.

Technically, all three national parks lie on the fringes of elk range, though the North Rim of Grand Canyon, and southern sections of Bryce Canyon produce far more sightings than Zion.

The most daunting physical characteristics of elk are their enormous frames. Mature bulls routinely attain weights of between 500 and 800 pounds and they stand five feet tall or higher at the shoulders. Cows weigh between 400 and 600 pounds and stand shorter.

The pelage of an elk is unmistakable, and is quite different from the grayish coat of a mule deer, which is far more commonly seen. An elk's head is dark brown. The bulk of its body color is tan, and the posterior area is creamy white. In fact, another colloquial name for elk—wapiti—owes its origin to Shawnee Indians whose word for elk literally means "white rump."

Sure indicators of elk presence are tracks—hoof prints—which are left behind in the mud and snow. The imprint resembles cloven half moons roughly four inches in diameter and far larger than those of a mule deer.

Perhaps the physical trait most synonymous with elk is the ornate growth of antlers on bulls. (Females, called cows, do not grow antlers.) These mighty protrusions are deciduous; they are shed every year usually by the end of March and subsequently a new set of antlers grows in their place. Once the antlers are dropped, fresh antler tines sprout as "velvet," so named because the surface of the emerging antlers is soft, velvet like, and underlain by a network of blood vessels and capillaries. Over the span of their 140-day development, antlers grow at a rate of about one-half inch per day, eventually reaching weights of up to 50 pounds and dimensions that may stretch two or three feet across. Toward the end of summer, the branches eventually harden, and bulls rub off the velvet overcoating in time for a mating ritual known as "the rut."

Autumn triggers a frenetic hormonal change within bulls. Visitors scouting forested areas of Grand Canyon's North Rim, for instance, may hear bull elk before they actually see them. Being polygamous, a single bull may recruit a dozen or more cows in his harem, but only after he has displayed his dominance over numerous male challengers. The rut begins in late summer and lasts through the first weeks of November. It is announced when bulls emit a high-pitched bugle that can be heard from miles away. Feverish jousting takes place as bulls lock antlers, using their sharpened tines as offensive and defensive tools.

The size of the antlers can help determine an animal's age. As a general rule of thumb, bulls between two and five years old carry racks with only a couple of tines on either side. From the fifth year through the age of nine, bulls often sport six tines on each side.

In late May and June, pregnant cows retreat to solitary places in the forest, where they give birth to calves. Following delivery, mothers and calves form nursery bands, which feed together and fend off predators such as mountain lions which have been known to prey upon juvenile animals.

Historically, the greatest threats to elk have not come from wildlife predators but from humans.

Overhunting during the early decades of the twentieth century eliminated elk from the Southwest. The wapiti which visitors see today are descendants of animals transplanted from Yellowstone National Park and other areas of the Rockies years ago. There is no precise estimate on the number of elk in the region.

Even though elk may appear docile and tame, never try to feed them. These animals are large, wild, and powerful. They also can be dangerous. Proceed with caution if you see an elk near the roadway, and never walk up to an animal that's grazing near your car. Cows are extremely protective of their calves, and bulls have been know to charge humans. Wildlife photographers should remember, too, that using artificial calls as a means of drawing elk closer is strictly prohibited in national parks. Park regulations require that people who are outside their vehicle must maintain a minimum viewing distance of at least 25 yards.

Where To Find Elk

Grand Canyon: Elk occasionally are viewed along Highway 67 leading to the Grand Canyon's North Rim from Jacob Lake to the North Rim Village. They are common at the South Rim.

Bryce Canyon: Elk are not viewed regularly within Bryce but between 100 and 150 individuals pass through the park seasonally. Historically as many as 17,000 elk used to range in the general vicinity of Bryce.

MULE DEER

Mule deer (*Odocoileus hemionus*) are the most abundant members of the deer family in the three national parks and often they can be viewed along the roadside. Close relatives of the white-tailed deer that are common throughout the lower 48 states, mule deer thrive in the arid, mountainous environment of the desert Southwest.

"Mulies" are somewhat larger and brawnier than the average white-tailed deer. While whitetails have tended to thrive alongside human development and agriculture, mule deer are foremost a species of the rugged wilderness. Still, these reclusive ungulates (hooved animals) have become so habituated to people that they are seen regularly in all three parks.

Although the males of both mule deer and elk sprout antlers, it's easy to distinguish one species from the other. Mule deer weigh roughly a third as much as an elk (males about 200 pounds, females 125 to 150 pounds), and there are key, corresponding differences in body shape, color, and antler size.

The light brown, almost tan, hair of the mule deer is evident on its back and forehead during the summer, but the hair becomes grayish brown in winter. The truly distinctive features of the deer are the black-tipped tail protruding from a whitish rump, and conspicuous, dull white patches inside its long ears, across its muzzle, and below the chin. Males, called bucks, grow beautiful sets of antlers that are nearly symmetrical. These branches are shed, however, in winter and a new growth starts to emerge a few months later.

A mule deer's frame is stocky, with muscles that carry the animal across steep inclines and habitat ranging from low-lying river bottoms and blackbrush valleys to open desert. Small bands of male deer will sometimes venture above the treeline in mid to late summer.

Mule deer subsist on a year-round diet of plants and brushy vegetation. In the summer, when wildflowers bloom, they will browse on cliffrose growing in the juniper-pinyon pine forest. Nomadic for much of the year, they sometimes assemble on winter ranges in a process known as "yarding up."

The time of courtship known as the rut commences in late October and early November; it casts dominant males into vigorous jousts for the right to breed with females. In June, following a gestation period of about 200 days, does give birth to fawns—

usually twins. Glands situated near the hooves on the mother's hind legs emit an odor that allows fawns to recognize their parent by virtue of her smell.

The primary predators of mule deer in the parks are mountain lions, coyotes, and bobcats.

Like elk, mule deer move to high elevations in the early summer and return to lowland areas during the winter. They do most of their foraging at night, so the prime time to go deer-watching is just after dawn and in the hours before dusk, although the deer in parks where they are not hunted can be seen any time of day.

Where To Find Mule Deer

Grand Canyon: They are common along roads, especially near railroad tracks in the village. Do not feed or pet (petting is considered molesting by park rangers).

Zion: An indication of the abundance of mule deer in Zion is a handwritten sign that was posted at the park's East Entrance recently: "Buckle Up, don't feed the deer. Have A Fun Day." Deer are ubiquitous in Zion and never far from rivers.

Bryce Canyon: Mulies are seen regularly along the park's interior road leading to Rainbow Point as well as forested sections Paunsaugunt Plateau and, of course, beneath the rim along backcountry trails.

DESERT BIGHORN SHEEP

There is nothing quite as regal as the sight of a bighorn sheep perched precariously on the ledge of a steep-faced mountain. The animal's innate beauty—accented by its mighty curl of horns—exudes the very feeling of rustic retreat that visitors try to find in national parks. And seeing a sheep dawdle expertly on the edge of doom, does not disappoint those who go bighorn watching with high expectations.

Desert bighorn sheep (*Ovis canadensis*) are a distinct variation—a subspecies—of the Rocky Mountain bighorn sheep, also known as "mountain sheep." Desert bighorns were extirpated from several areas of the national parks by hunters earlier in this century and have since made a comeback through reintroduction efforts. In the parks they live in a harsh, wind-blown environment where temperatures fluctuate between searing heat and bitter cold.

A bighorn's body generally is brownish-tan in color, though in some cases individual animals may appear dark gray, or even tawny if they are in areas where the hair has been bleached by the sun. Regardless of body color, however, all bighorns have a white rump patch and whitish coloration around the nose. Bighorns also are defined by their stout, muscular frames that allow for sprinting across steep slopes with a low center of gravity. They weigh between 125 and 300 pounds.

A sheep's hooves are critical to its navigational prowess. The hooves are hard-edged, yet each one has a soft sole that provides grip on the rocks. The sharp nature of the hooves makes them effective weapons against mountain lions. Bestowed with good eyesight and keen hearing, sheep are timid animals that maintain a distance between their bands and wilderness predators.

Rams roam separately except during the breeding season, which usually occurs in December. With it comes a dramatic, head-butting lesson in wildlife behavior. Mature rams face off and crack their horns in a test of dominance at speeds of up to 40 miles per hour. Some visitors have heard the jarring cracks of impact for as much as a mile away.

The winner earns the right to mate with ewes which give birth to lambs about 5 1/2 months later, usually in June. The more sociable female sheep congregate in small herds, which makes them easy to locate in the spring and summer, when they form nursery bands to raise their young. The group is led by an elder matriarch.

Before spotting bighorns you might first see tracks in the sand. They appear as double lobes resembling teardrops about 3 to 3 1/2 inches long; they are similar to a mule deer's prints but straighter and less curved on the outside.

After bighorns feed on grasses, they can often be seen resting and simply chewing their cud. Healthy bighorns are fairly long lived, reaching documented ages of at least 15 years. According to park officials, the primary cause of mortality is disease, including pinkeye which can lead to blindness or pneumonia.

Desert bighorns have survived only because they retreat to craggy points and rock outcroppings that are beyond reach of most predators, including humans. Natural predators include coyotes, golden eagles—which are capable of plucking young lambs from the high ramparts—mountain lions and bobcats—which wait in ambush.

In marked contrast to elk and deer, both sexes of bighorn sheep have horns that continue to grow from their heads for their entire lives. While the C-shaped spirals that protrude from the heads of male bighorns are better recognized, females have horns rising like straight spikes eight to ten inches long. Because of this, ewes bear a strong resemblance to mountain goats, which are not found in the region.

On adult male sheep, the horns generally do not achieve full curls until the animal reaches eight years of age. Outside the national parks, bighorns are prized by hunters but inside the parks they are afforded sanctuary. Nevertheless, poaching has been a persistent problem and visitors who see suspicious activity should notify park officials at once.

Where To Find Desert Bighorn Sheep

The premier place for spotting bighorns within the three parks mentioned in this book are the bottom of the Grand Canyon along the Colorado River. River rafting guides well acquainted with local fauna are able to point out the steep headwalls tumbling off the canyon rim where bighorns frequent. They are also commonly seen just below the rim along West Rim Drive and in the village area. The species was extirpated but reintroduced to Zion.

BADGER

Pound for pound, there are few predators that match a badger's persistence in stalking its prey. These members of the weasel family are not only powerful digging machines but their perceived aggressiveness is legendary. To locate a likely place for badgers to live, first try to find a thriving population of animals which they like to feed on—ground squirrels, pocket gophers, or prairie dogs.

Being nomadic in the sense that it will follow communities of rodents as they shift across the landscape, the badger (*Taxidea taxus*) typically makes its home in open meadows. The physique and markings of a badger are striking. The design of its body is low to the ground yet imposing. Look for a line of white under a badger's snout, vertically across its flattened head, and along its upper backbone. The badger also is decorated with a patch of white fur on both cheeks and ears, broken only by a hook-shaped pattern of dark brown that is similar to sideburns. Its back is marbled gray and brown.

A carnivore with extraordinary strength for its size (it weighs only 30 pounds), its long claws make it masterfully equipped to dig out a new den or perhaps bulldoze its way into a ground squirrel burrow to retrieve a meal.

Generally, badgers are nocturnal (night foraging), but due to the absence of human hunting of badgers inside national parks, those in Grand Canyon, Zion, and Bryce are more tolerant of people and, as a result, are active during all hours of the day. Despite the badger's habit of simply leaving its victims' bones and hair outside the den, it pays close attention to its own grooming, both licking its coat clean and burying its own scat.

Badgers usually are left alone by other predators though there have been instances in the wild where a badger and coyote will work cooperatively to hunt elusive prey. As a badger digs its way into the den of a ground squirrel, a coyote will sometimes wait outside the den's alternate escape hatch.

Where To Find Badgers

Wherever you find stable populations of ground squirrels and other rodents that live in open scrub and grasslands, that is where you will find badgers. Ask at park visitor centers for the latest location of badger dens but never approach them within 25 yards because the animals can be aggressive.

PORCUPINE

The porcupine (*Erethizon dorsatum*) is as shy as its quills are worthy of respect. It is a species that seeks no malice but when some is provided by either a predator or troublemaker this animal is there reluctantly to proffer a response. Of course, this timid, prickly-pear mammal—the only species of its kind in North America—is widely recognized for its sharp armor.

An adult carries up to 30,000 spiny quills in his bodily quiver; however, contrary to popular belief, a porcupine cannot shoot its quills into an attacker. Rather, the quills are earned by any animal that puts an unwanted nose or paw into the porcupine's guard hairs. The quills are quite easily released from a porcupine's coat, but it is far more difficult to remove the sharp barbs from an impaled victim. It is a good reason pet owners should leave their dogs at home when planning to visit porcupine country.

Porcupines prefer to stay in the pine woodlands and willow thickets found at mid to lower elevations. Wobbly in its gait, porcupines are surprisingly adept at scaling trees. They have soft underbellies and yellowstone-brown guard hairs covering the quills on their backs.

Male porcupines are solitary until the autumn mating period, when they join females and engage in high-pitched squealing during courtship. Well nourished adult animals can attain weights of between 35 and 40 pounds. Following a gestation period of about seven months, one baby is born with a full set of quills which are soft at birth but harden within hours.

One sure sign of porcupine presence is the trademark paw prints, which look as if the bottom of the feet were dobbled in pebbles. Marks from their long claws are usually visible also. Another sign of porcupine activity is a tree with its bark pulled away from the trunk and tooth marks left in place of the bark. Porcupines eat bark and complement their diet with twigs, leaves, lupine, and other plants.

The animal also has a taste for salt that can become lethal. The national parks do not use salt on the icy winter roads but elsewhere many porcupines feeding on road salt are killed by passing automobiles. Predators of the porcupine include coyotes, mountain lions, and bobcats. The average lifespan of a healthy adult is seven to eight years.

Where To Find Porcupines

Porcupines are common throughout all three parks, mostly at higher elevations in pinyon-juniper-oak forests and Ponderosa pine that begins above 4,000 feet.

BEAVER

Beavers are there all right, swishing around in the Colorado River and some of its connecting tributaries. But nowadays with the dams along the Colorado controlling stream flows on such a wide, deep river, even natural engineers such as beaver would have a difficult time wielding a major influence compared to massive walls of concrete and steel that hold rivers back.

Nonetheless, beavers (*Castor canadensis*) are builders of wetland complexes even in dry, desert environments which gives them a prominent place. The number of beavers that occupied the interiors of Grand Canyon, Zion, and Bryce before fur trappers seriously depleted their numbers is anyone's guess. There is persistent talk of reintroducing the beaver to stream systems as a means of helping to protect riparian ecosystems and that may soon come to pass as scientists continue to fully understand the benefits that beavers bring.

With resilient, bucked teeth, a beaver chews the trunk of a tree to a conical point, fells it, then uses the log as material for a dam or spherical lodge. As the largest rodent in North America, the beaver is ideally adapted to water. It employs its flat, paddle-like tail to navigate the water; its heavy, waterproof fur insulates the animal from winter cold; and it has valves that prevent water from entering its nose and ears.

In places where beaver are viewed as anathema to agriculture, they have been shot or removed. In the three parks, they contend only with natural predators such as coyotes, bobcats, mountain lions, and foxes, which will kill a beaver if they find it on land. If a beaver is startled by human presence, the animal will slap its tail down on the water and dive out of sight. Beavers are most active on the fringes of daylight around dawn and dusk.

Where To Find Beavers

Grand Canyon: In the Colorado River and a few of its tributaries.

Zion: Along the Virgin River where you likely will see evidence of beaver activity by gnawed cottonwoods.

Bryce Canyon: Beavers have been extirpated from Bryce though there are indications the rodents might be attempting to recolonize riverways near the park. Beavers are present in the Tropic Reservoir beyond the park's western boundary and in the East Fork of the Sevier River.

RINGTAIL

Although their colloquial names imply that they are felines, ringtails (*Bassariscus astutus*) are closer in their origin to common raccoons than wildcats. And few creatures have made better mousers—which explains how these fixtures of Grand Canyon, Zion, and Bryce Canyon acquired their identity.

Interestingly enough, ringtails are members of the family Procyonidae which gives them kindredness, at least in scientific grouping, with the Asian panda, the olingos of Latin America, and yes, the common raccoon. This family of omnivores (meat and plant eaters) are known for their long tails and contrasting ring-like tail bands. Whereas the dark tail stripes and bandit mask on a raccoon are conspicuous, with ringtails it is almost as if the colors have been reversed. They have a grayish-brown body like a raccoon's but with a white bandit mask (eye rings) that encircles big, dark eyes, and a long tail that is highlighted by its white stripes which almost appear to glow. Some have labeled them a cross between a fox's sleek body, a housecat's face, and a raccoon's markings.

Curious and nocturnal, emboldened by past successes, ringtails have shown their adroitness at raiding campsites, which is why hikers should maintain clean camps and refrain from feeding these nighttime visitors. If cornered, the ringtail is likely to appear formidably fierce so it is a good idea not to pursue them. Like mink, skunks, and a host of other animals that secrete musky liquid from their anal glands when they feel threatened, ringtails deliver a similar spray. Their bite and sharp claws are tools that must also be respected.

As long as there has been human habitation in the desert Southwest, ringtails probably played a role by feeding upon discarded garbage. In more recent times, they earned the nickname "Miner's Cat" because humans living in miner's camps actually welcomed ringtails, acknowledging their skill at catching mice and other unwanted rodents. True scavengers, ringtails take advantage of whatever is available—and in the desert there is a veritable smorgasbord of possibilities: rodents, snakes and lizards, frogs, scorpions and other insects, rabbits, and birds.

The hunting methods of ringtails are rather sobering. They, like other creatures that hunt in the night, will lie in wait along a game trail and ambush their smaller prey by first pouncing upon it with extending front paws and then dispatching the surprised victim with a bite to the neck.

Ringtails, like raccoons, also appear to be fastidious in their grooming, washing their paws and fur by streamside. During cold spells, ringtails may become dormant and set up a den in a hollow log, rockpile or underground burrow. Mating takes place in early spring and a litter of between two and four young are born six to eight weeks later.

Where To Find Ringtails

In all three parks, ringtails are found in the lower elevation cliff and riparian areas, although with their nocturnal feeding habits they are not seen often.

KAIBAB AND ABERT'S SQUIRREL

Geologically speaking, it might be considered merely a few ticks on the clock of time, but evolutionary scientists say the divergence of Kaibab and Abert's squirrels may be as old as the making of the Grand Canyon itself. Eons ago, before erosion gouged out the main rifts of the canyon, it is likely a single species of tassel-eared squirrel inhabited the coniferous subalpine forests that stretched across what is today the intersection of southern Utah and northern Arizona. But as the two sides of the canyon grew farther apart, distinct subspecies emerged—the Kaibab (*Sciurus kaibabensis*), which is listed as an endangered species and found today on the North Rim; and the more common Abert's (*Sciurus aberti*) which resides in forests along the South Rim.

Kaibab Squirrel

In behavior they are remarkably similar but coloration distinguishes them. The Abert's has grizzled gray fur on its back, a white underbelly and a fluffy, grizzled tail. The telltale physical characteristic of this squirrel, however, is its unmistakable long, tassel-like hairs which explains why it is known colloquially as "the tassel-eared squirrel."

The Kaibab, on the other hand and literally on the other side of the rim, bears only a passing resemblance to the Abert's. It is impossible to miss the Kaibab's white ears and fluffy white tail which might cause some to believe they are seeing a skunk climbing through the pines. The Kaibab has dark gray fur on top as well as along its belly. It does not flaunt the obvious ear tassels evident on its cousin.

Both squirrels make their nests in tree crotches high above the ground and similarly they strip pine cones of their seeds and supplement their diet with the cambium layer of tree bark and various plants and berries. Food is cached underground and eaten later. The primary predators of both squirrels are raptors—goshawks and owls.

Other true squirrel species which might be in the same general area are the red squirrel (*Tamiascirus hudsonicus*) also known as the "chickaree;" and the rock squirrel (*Spermophilus variegatus*). Red squirrels, identified by their rust-colored coats, are roughly a third the size of the Kaibab and Abert's. Rock squirrels, which are grizzled gray and ground dwelling, are abundant in rocky areas in all three parks.

The Kaibab is unique to the Kaibab Plateau and found nowhere else. It is listed as an endangered species and afforded special protection because of its limited range and threats to that range which include extensive logging that has occurred on the plateau.

The Abert's, meanwhile, is found across Arizona, New Mexico, and Colorado. These squirrels also can be viewed to the east side of Rocky Mountain National Park.

Abert's Squirrel

Where To Find Kaibab and Abert's Squirrels

On the North Rim: Kaibab squirrels are relatively abundant on the North Rim and a quiet, patient walk through the open forest is likely to yield opportunities to view these intriguing rodents. Although the North Rim is closed to winter visitation, the Kaibabs stay active year-round, breeding in late winter and giving birth to a litter of young about a month later.

On the South Rim: Abert's squirrels can be found in Ponderosa and pinyon pines.

UTAH WHITE-TAILED PRAIRIE DOG

Limited to a very small range, the Utah white-tailed prairie dog (*Cynomys parvidens*), a native of Bryce Canyon National Park, is considered a conservation success story and appears to be bouncing back after coming dangerously close to total annihilation. Here, you can have the satisfaction of seeing a threatened species in clear view along the roadside and be given the chance to observe the role that it plays in nature—as an animal that sustains other critters by being eaten.

They may not be as glamorous as a mountain lion or elk but prairie dogs assume several prominent roles in the wild. For certain raptors (birds of prey) and small carnivores, they are a principle source of food. For wildlife watchers, they are delightful, social rodents to observe. And for ranchers and farmers, they are considered the bane of crops and livestock.

The latter is why prairie dogs throughout the American West

79

have been treated with the same respect accorded noxious weeds and why most of the five species of prairie dogs are in trouble biologically, due to poisoning, trapping, and shooting. As early as the 1950s, biologists knew they were skidding toward extinction and 20 years later an aggressive program was under-way to save them.

Today, the national park offers the premier viewing opportu-nities for these skittish rodents in the country. Their small "towns" are abuzz with frenetic activity and by witnessing them one can only imagine what the western plains must have looked like when prairie dog colonies spread themselves across millions of acres.

You will be able to identify the encampments of Utah dogs by their earth-disturbing mounds which are built around a network of underground tunnels and dens.

Utah dogs breed in March after going underground in October to escape the coldest span of winter. To sustain them-selves they rely upon thick layers of body fat that are built up over the summer and fall. After four months of napping as a means of conserving energy, females give birth to between four and six pups that reside underground for a couple weeks and then emerge to the world at spring's end. Their whole universe consists of meadows with grass not too tall and yet loaded with edible stalks and woody forbs. If a Utah prairie dog is successful at evading predators and surviving the winter, an adult may achieve a lifespan of five years or more.

A host of predators make prairie dog towns a regular hunting stop. Badgers are known to set up their dens on the edge of prairie dog communities and actually move with the prey species as the network of burrows and dens expands. Coyotes will not pass up a meal if the opportunity presents itself and a number of predatory birds, including hawks, owls, and eagles, will swoop in on an unsuspecting dog. Although Bryce Canyon is located high above the Utah desert, rattlesnakes occasionally slither into town and grab one as a snack as well.

Of course, the prairie dogs have prepared themselves by setting up a warning system based on vocalizations that are expressed by sentinels which warn the rest of the community if an invader approaches.

The Utah prairie dogs in Bryce Canyon have been used in transplantation projects elsewhere and this population is considered a vital reservoir for recovery of the species. In recent years, the number of prairie dogs has waxed and waned. Their numbers are currently declining.

Where to Find Utah White-tailed Prairie Dogs

Bryce Canyon National Park is considered a principle recovery area for these threatened animals. There are established colonies north of the Sunset Campground and southwest of the Visitor Center. They are also seen in the forest clearings in the northern end of the park.

BAT

Bats are not birds but flying mammals of the order *Chiroptera*. The Colorado Plateau country, with its endless labyrinth of canyons, caves, rock overhangs, and insects is one reason it is highly productive terrain for bats. Among the 20 or so species of bats that can be found in the vicinity of Grand Canyon, Zion, and Bryce the Western pipistrelle (*Pipistrellus hesperus*) is the most common. There are a half-dozen other bat species that deserve mention: the Yuma Myotis (*Myotis yumanensis*), long-legged Myotis (*Myotis volans*), California Myotis (*Myotis californicus*), the big brown bat (*Eptesicus fuscus*), the Western small-footed Myotis (*Myotis ciliobrum*) and the pallid bat (*Antrozous pallidus*). They are all part of the family of plainnose bats—as opposed to those classified as free-tails—and their abundance is determined by average mean temperature, altitude and type of terrain. The silver-haired bat (*Lasionycteris noctivagans*), for example, is common in higher elevations in the parks while the big brown bat is common in lower elevations such as the bottom of the Grand Canyon.

The difference between plainnose bats, which belong to the family *Vespertilionidae*, and free-tailed bats, from the family *Molossidae*, is that the wing membranes on free-tails does not extend to the tip of the tail. It makes little difference in their ability to flicker through the night and catch insects, however.

People have an irrational fear of bats and the chance that bats might get caught in your hair is highly unlikely. The expression "blind as a bat" is really a misnomer because bats can see, but they rely on what is know as echolocation to hunt. This is done by emitting supersonic sounds which bounce back from objects as they fly. From their sophisticated ability to read variations in returning frequency, they can decipher whether the object in front of them is a bug or canyon wall. While bats have suffered from a bad reputation, they have been helpful to humans by eating enormous amounts of mosquitoes and other insects.

Western pipistrelles are the smallest bat found in the parks and weigh about as much as a key. They and other bats are so proficient at catching and eating bugs that they are thought to consume as much as 30 to 50 percent of their body weight in insects each night. According to one estimate, a colony of bats might consume several hundred tons of insects over the course of a year. As you walk in the cool night air of the park, thank the bats for not having to douse yourself with insect repellent.

"Bats are important indicators of a healthy environment, and they should be a welcome part of our neighborhoods," writes renowned bat expert Merlin D. Tuttle in his book *America's Neighborhood Bats.* "Like canaries in a mine, they serve as early warning systems for dangerous high pesticide and pollution levels...Their presence is clearly beneficial—they will leave you alone, but mosquitoes won't!"

Where To Find Bats

These flying mammals are ubiquitous and can be seen in most open areas of the national parks at dusk. The best viewing locations are along open canyon areas.

RIVER OTTER

Historically, river otters were native to the Colorado River drainage, but because no formal count has been taken it is uncertain how many of these animals remain today. It is a known fact, however, that trapping took a toll on these furbearing members of the mink family and a compelling question now is whether the surviving ones can rebound or whether the federal government should try to restore otters artificially to their former haunts.

River otters (*Lutra canadensis*) are the second largest members of the weasel family in North America and they are a delight to watch. Their long, slender frames are effectively water-dynamic. Using their furry tails as rudders, their webbed feet as propulsion aids, and their nasal valve system to prevent water from entering the nostrils, otters are excellent swimmers. They need considerable agility in order to catch trout, frogs, and other prey.

Male otters grow to lengths of four feet, and attain weights of nearly 25 pounds (females slightly less). Otters have special adaptations for reproduction. Although mating occurs in the spring, development of embryos (usually twins) is delayed until winter. The young are born in March or April, nearly a year after conception took place.

Two indicators of otter presence are five-toed tracks in the mud that usually reflect the animal's webbed feet, and greenish scat (fecal droppings) laced with fish bones or scales. Making their home beneath a riverbank or the shoreline of a pond, otters dig permanent dens that are accessible through underwater lanes called "runs." River otters are active both day and night.

Where To Find River Otters

In the Grand Canyon, river otters have been spotted infrequently by floaters on the Colorado River.

AMPHIBIANS

CANYON TREEFROG

The canyon treefrog (*Hyla arenicolor*) is the most common frog species that visitors are likely to see in the national parks because many of the roadways, trails, and campsites are located near stream corridors where they live. In the coolness of night, you may actually be alerted to their presence first by their sonorous croaking. The frog is characterized by colors that vary between olive, gray, or brown with discernible dark patches on its back, and an eye stripe. They measure between 1¼ inches and 2¼ inches in length and can usually be seen among riparian tree species such as willow, cottonwood, tamarisk, and cedar. They are not poisonous. The prime predators of treefrogs are snakes, lizards, birds, ringtails, and skunks. The canyon treefrog is among eight species of amphibians found in Grand Canyon and six in Zion.

Where To Find Canyon Treefrogs

They can be seen at the bottom of the Grand Canyon around shallow pools near the Colorado River, and in canyons throughout Zion.

GREAT BASIN SPADEFOOT TOAD

Three other amphibians—the Great Basin spadefoot toad (*Scaphiopus intermontanus*), the red-spotted toad (*Bufo punctatus*) and the Rocky Mountain toad (*Bufo woodhousei woodhousei*)—are found in the same type of habitat as the treefrog and during a walk along a river you are as likely to see a toad as a frog.

Here are a few suggestions for telling them apart. The Great Basin spadefoot has a distinctive "hourglass" marking that is gray or olive on its back and accented by light gray streaks. It takes its name from the wedge-shaped spade on its hind feet. The Red-spotted toad is roughly the same size as the spadefoot and is defined by its gray to reddish-brown coloring and reddish warts. It has a flat head and pointed snout. The Rocky Mountain toad is more abundant in Grand Canyon than in Zion.

The spadefoot has an interesting natural history. After laying its eggs in the sand, they might remain dormant for months until sufficient rain creates conditions for the tadpoles to thrive. Spring and summer storms can spawn what seems like an overnight emergence of spadefoot tadpoles in the dry slick-rock creek beds. In Bryce Canyon in wet years this phenomenon can be witnessed near the headwaters of East Creek flowing off the Paunsaugunt Plateau between Inspiration Point and Paria View and in the streams flowing into the East Fork of the Sevier River along the park's western border.

Where To Find Great Basin Spadefoot Toads

They are common in the desert regions of the Grand Canyon and Zion where there is water. In Bryce they are found near springs and in marshes.

TIGER SALAMANDER

Distributed across much of the United States, tiger salamanders (*Ambystoma tigrinum*) are found from sea level to 11,000 feet. In all three parks, they similarly exist at most elevations. Salamanders look like a cross between a frog and a reptile, but biologically they are more kindred to the former. They are amphibians, which means they are adept at environments. From May through August tiger salamanders are in the process of metamorphic transition. After they hatch, the larvae swim as tadpoles in seasonal, fishless ponds and marshlands along rivers. At adulthood, these salamanders can be quite large—between three and eight inches long—and will be identified by their small broad heads, brown eyes, and bodies with yellow or dull green patches.

Park visitors in summer commonly see tiger salamanders,

especially after evening rains when they emerge from damp underground burrows that afford them sanctuary from the heat of the day. Non-poisonous, they feed upon insects, worms, small frogs, and even infant mice. In turn, a number of bird, mammal and snake species eat them. In Zion and Grand Canyon, they occur as a subspecies called the Arizona tiger salamander (*Ambystoma tigrinum nebulosum*) and are easily identified by dark yellowish-green blotches.

Where To Find Tiger Salamanders

Grand Canyon: In the tadpole stage they are abundant in the seasonal ponds that flank the roadside leading to the North Rim south of Jacob Lake.

Zion: They are present along the Virgin River and in back-country pools that hold water.

Bryce: Look for them in the vicinity of Swamp Canyon and near springs seeping out from the ground, both above and below the rim.

REPTILES

SHORT-HORNED LIZARD

Most people know short-horned lizards by their popular name which is simply "horny toad." These small reptiles frequent higher elevations in all three parks, generally in the vicinity of pinyon-juniper forest and Ponderosa pine. Mountain short-horns (*Phrynosoma douglassi*) are likely to be seen darting among rocks and shifting patterns of shade. Like most lizards, they are skittish and able to flee in the blink of an eye.

Cold-blooded animals are extremely sensitive to changes in ambient temperature, and cold spells make them sluggish, which

Previous pages' photograph: Northern Sagebrush Lizards

is why they are most active during the spring, summer, and autumn. Horny toads actively seek surfaces that are warmed by the sun. The heat allows their blood to flow easier and as a result they are far more agile and less exposed to predators. An amazing survival tool short-horns have is their ability to shoot blood from their eyes at animals that are threatening them.

Short-horns are distinguished by a flat body and short tail but the most obviously physical characteristic is their short row of horns running down the spine and back of the head. The color of their skin can actually change slightly between a dark gray and an almost sandy hue depending on the temperature. They are chameleon like, in that their skin color can change to match their surroundings.

A mother short-horn carries eggs inside her body and releases them only when they are about to hatch. Scientists say that as many as two dozen babies may be born.

Where To Find Short-horned Lizards

In all parks, short-horned lizards can be found simply by staking out rock piles and simply waiting for them to appear.

GRAND CANYON AND GREAT BASIN RATTLESNAKE

There are at least six snake species in the parks that are members of the pit viper (*Crotalinae*) family, which means that they are poisonous. Among those that visitors to Bryce Canyon and Zion are likely to see is the Great Basin rattlesnake (*Crotalus viridis lutosus*) and the Grand Canyon rattlesnake (*Crotalus viridis abyssus*) which is found in Grand Canyon and nowhere else. Both of these rattlesnakes are a subspecies of the widely distributed Western rattlesnake.

The Grand Canyon rattler is light brown, almost tan, in color with blotches that are found on most rattlesnakes. These blotches are dark, and irregularly shaped with pale centers. Adults achieve lengths of almost three feet. Lying in ambush, it feeds on

Grand Canyon Rattlesnake

rodents and insects, debilitating larger prey by puncturing the skin with its fangs and injecting venom into the wound.

Generally, it will coil into a mass and rattle its tail if disturbed. Hikers aren't likely to encounter the Grand Canyon rattler on established trails as the serpent tends to position itself under logs or rock piles where it can forage and not be disturbed. Those who venture off trail and bushwack should use care and watch their step.

The Great Basin rattler is also brownish in color with brown blotches across its back. It is the only poisonous reptile in Bryce and has been known to be a predator of Utah prairie dogs. Inhabiting forests as well as the desert canyon country, it is aggressive if cornered and can achieve a length of five feet.

Experts say that snakes are far more likely to strike in hot conditions, particularly when the temperature is above 74 degrees Fahrenheit. Of course, it is obvious that snakes should be let alone and under no circumstances should you try to catch a snake or any other animal in the parks. A pit viper produces a poisonous venom that can be treated with antivenin serum.

Where To Find Rattlesnakes

The Grand Canyon rattlesnake's chief habitat is desert scrub country and stream sides within the canyon itself.

The Great Basin rattler is found above and below the rim of Bryce Canyon and throughout Zion.

COLLARED LIZARD

While visitors are likely to see the mountain short-horned lizard at higher elevations on the Colorado Plateau, the collared lizard (*Crotaphytuscollaris baileyi*) will be found at hotter, lower elevations. Collared lizards are jerky in their movements across rocks and can disappear in an instant. If you have an opportunity to see a collared lizard, one of the first details you will notice is the long tail that can extend twice the length of the body. It tends to have a flat back that is marked by two black bands in the shoulder region.

As ambient temperature changes, sometimes the overall color of a collared lizard will change too, fluctuating between a pale green and light brown. The lizard, at adulthood, attains a length of between three and four inches. Surviving off insects, the lizard is not poisonous and poses no threat to humans.

Other lizards that may be found nearby are the yellowback spiny lizard (*Sceloporus magister uniformis*) which has a hulking physique that can reach 5 1/2 inches long. The colorful markings of this lizard include green, yellow, and brown and metallic blue over a generally light gray or brown body. There are also black markings apparent in the shoulder area.

A third common species is the whiptail of which there are several subspecies. These lizards are, like the spiny, light gray or brown. There also are two subspecies of the Plateau lizard, the northern variation occupying higher elevations in Zion, Bryce, and the North Rim. On the floor of the Grand Canyon, hikers may see the Western whiptail.

All lizards that you may encounter in the parks are carnivores, except for the chuckwalla found in Grand Canyon. It is an herbivore.

Where To Find Collared Lizards

They are found chiefly in open, rocky terrain usually on the sides of large boulders, and also on rocks that sit at the edge of streams.

Gopher Snake

WHIPSNAKE AND GOPHER SNAKE

While rattlesnakes and other poisonous reptiles transfix the attention of visitors, it should be noted that wildlife watchers interested in observing the slithering park inhabitants stand a far better chance of seeing snakes that are not venomous. Perhaps the two most common harmless snakes in the Grand Canyon and Zion environs are the desert striped whipsnake (*Masticophis taeniatus taeniatus*) native to desert scrub country, and the Sonoran gopher snake (*Pituophis melanoleucus affinis*) which inhabits drier areas of the park.

The desert striped whipsnake has four narrow stripes running the entire length of its dark body which is slender compared to the stout physiques of rattlesnakes. This critter also is longer than most other snake kin achieving maximum lengths of six feet, though three to four feet is standard. The

97

Sonoran gopher snake, found in Grand Canyon, is similar to the Great Basin gopher snake (*Pituophis melanoleucus diserticola*) and in fact is an evolutionary offshoot. These too can reach lengthy dimensions— between three and six feet in length—marked by reddish or yellowish skin, with dark blotches down the back and a dark line that extends from one eye to the other.

Where To Find Snakes

Hikers have seen these snakes along many trails in the parks.

DESERT TORTOISE

The desert tortoise (*Gopherus agassizii*) has been in the public eye because the species is in a dangerous decline due to development and destruction of its habitat. A dryland species that ranges across open desert scrub, the tortoise so declined in its numbers that the federal government afforded the species full protection under the Endangered Species Act. In the wild it is instantly recognizable by its dark, domed shell that is ornamented by rough rectangular creases. From head to posterior, adults can achieve lengths of 15 inches and some have compared the slow-moving creature's legs to those of an elephant.

Where To Find Desert Tortoises

Desert tortoises have occurred within 55 miles of Zion National Park at lower elevations. They also are not officially listed as a native species by Grand Canyon officials though scientists say all three parks lie so close to ideal tortoise range that it is possible they might occur in the parks.

GILA MONSTER

Another reptile of note and one that enters into the legends of Native Americans is the banded gila (pronounced Hee-Luh) monster (*Heloderma suspectum cinctum*) which is a member of the family *Helodermatidae*. The gila monster can be irrascible if it is cornered and will emit a fierce hissing sound. The display is impressive coming from a plump animal that is about a foot long. It is the only known poisonous lizard in the world. Very colorful, it has a thick tail that seems to have beads on it and the body has banded shades of orange, yellow, black, and pink. The animal poses no threat to humans as long as they are left alone. If provoked, it will bite and inject a poisonous venom into the wound. It is a close cousin to the reticulate gila monster, which also has a thick skin.

Where To Find Gila Monsters

They are extremely rare but known to inhabit rocky strips along streams where there is creosotebush, in effect near water where the insects they feed upon gather.

BIRDS

BALD EAGLE

Besides being America's national wildlife symbol, bald eagles (*Haliaeetus leucocephalus*) are considered by many scientists to be true indicators of a clean and healthy environment. While bald eagles use the three national parks as wintering or stopover areas following their autumn southward migration from Canada and the northern United States, few, if any, of the large raptors breed or reside permanently in the region. Nonetheless, during the winter and spring months when bald eagles from farther south start heading north, these birds of prey are common.

Bald eagles have been imprinted upon the American conscience for more than two centuries. In 1782 Congress selected the bald eagle as the national symbol over the objections of

Benjamin Franklin who wanted instead to honor the wild turkey. Franklin argued that the eagle's reputation and lifestyle was not noble enough but few today would maintain that Congress made the wrong choice. When perched in a tree, a majestic, full-grown eagle stands between 2 1/2 and 3 feet tall; when cruising over a waterway, its extended wings span six to seven feet and command awe. They also are gifted with incredible eyesight. One researcher noted that a bald eagle spotted another eagle flying 20 miles away.

As everyone familiar with the species knows, bald eagles are not truly bald. Their name is derived from the Greek *leucocephalus*, meaning "white-headed." The bird's crown and tail feathers take on their famed snow-white hue only when it reaches adulthood. The process of maturation takes four to five years and involves five distinct molts (feather sheddings). In the meantime, observers unfamiliar with the brown phase markings of immature bald eagles often confuse them with golden eagles, which do reside and breed in mountainous backcountry areas of the parks.

During the 1950s and 1960s when use of the pesticide DDT was widespread, the number of birds declined sharply due to the fact that the chemical affected a bird's ability to lay eggs that could produce a healthy embryo. Even though DDT was banned permanently in 1972, the bald eagle was given status as an endangered species, prompting aggressive action to secure eagle habitat. A few decades later, the work apparently has paid off. The federal government has down-graded the status of eagles from endangered to threatened based on the fact that numbers of breeding pairs of eagles are increasing.

Where To Find Bald Eagles

Grand Canyon: There are a few nesting pairs of bald eagles that make their nests inside the Grand Canyon. During the late autumn and winter months, floaters and hikers regularly will see them perched in trees at the river's edge or flying through the canyon.

105

Zion: Eagles sometimes can be seen from late autumn into the early spring months along the Virgin River which is flanked by Zion Canyon Scenic Drive.

Bryce Canyon: Bald eagles can be seen feasting upon dead animals that have been struck by cars inside the park. If you're traveling to the park in the winter, ask rangers if they know of any recent eagle sightings.

RED-TAILED HAWK

The red-tailed hawk (*Buteo jamaicensis*) is the second most abundant raptor, after the great horned owl, in the parks. Redtails reside in the parks year-round, breeding and wintering. In general redtails are less wary of humans than golden eagles, peregrine falcons, and other birds of prey. They hunt for rodents over every type of habitat except open water and at all elevations. Active through the day, they provide wildlife watchers with an intimate glimpse at the predator-prey relationship.

A redtail's wingspan measures four feet or more, and its markings are hard to miss. The adult is adorned with brownish feathers on top and a reddish (rufous) tail with a brown strip that runs parallel to the bird's body. From the ground as the bird floats overhead, you can see the redtail's lighter, rust-colored tail; its off-white under belly decorated with wavy bands of brown; and the brown patches on its head. The same brown is present laterally across the shoulders and again on the wingtips.

Three commonly seen hawks which primarily inhabit the deep forest are the Northern Goshawk, the Sharp-shinned Hawk and the Cooper's Hawk. The latter is the most common but all three breed and are permanent residents of the parks at high elevations. Four nesting pairs are known to feed inside the park.

Where To Find Red-tailed Hawks

If the red-tailed hawk isn't soaring above a meadow or open

forest, you'll see it perched in a tree, watching for movement on the ground with its razor-sharp eyesight.

Sightings of goshawks have occurred along both rims of the Grand Canyon where they prey upon Kaibab, Abert's, and red squirrels. They also can be seen in forests at Bryce. In Zion, they are common along cliff faces and in meadows.

Red-tailed Hawk

GOLDEN EAGLE

The golden eagle is irregularly spotted in all three parks. These efficient hunters make their home in the park year round, as opposed to the bald eagle which is merely a seasonal inhabitant.

The golden eagle (*Aquila chrysaetos*) is named for its "golden" (actually dark brown) head feathers. They are distinguished from bald eagles in that they hunt primarily over land, rather than water—and in the desert Southwest, except for the man-made lakes created by the damming of the Colorado River, large open bodies of water are scarce. That's why the vast spread of scrub, sage, and rocks is attractive to the golden eagle where its chief prey—rabbits, small rodents, even deer fawns—are accessible to pluck with their talons.

These birds strike an imposing presence in the sky as they soar with seven-foot wingspans and will chase their prey in dives that reach speeds of 100 miles per hour. By using their keen eyesight, equal to seven-power binoculars, and their incredible maneuverability, golden eagles can spot prey from hundreds of feet above the ground.

During the 1960s the number of golden eagles declined, as did other raptor populations, primarily due to the pervasive use of the pesticide DDT. Today golden eagle numbers appear to have stabilized within the parks, but the species, like the bald eagle, remains protected by federal law.

When identifying golden eagles, look first to the color of the feathers, then to the head. In differentiating between goldens and immature bald eagles, consider the type of terrain. Bald eagles congregate around water, while golden eagles inhabit country that is drier and more open.

From the ground, the outline of a golden eagle resembles that of a hawk. The adult golden's full brown plumage is achieved when the bird is about four years old, following two or three moltings (feather sheddings). Despite the raptor's reputation among sheep ranchers for killing young lambs, goldens will hunt wildlife such as ground squirrels, marmots, rabbits, reptiles, and prairie dogs if available. Much of the golden's bad press has been exaggerated.

During the spring breeding and nesting season, goldens demand solitude. They build their nests out of sticks and twigs placed on a high rock ledge or at the top of a pine. The female generally lays two whitish eggs. Successful production of offspring is influenced by the weather. Spring storms and high winds have been known to take their toll on young birds before they're able to fledge. It's vitally important to minimize human intrusion during the nesting season.

Where To Find Golden Eagles

They may be seen around the steep red rock cliffs that are so visible from scenic overlooks.

PEREGRINE FALCON

The rugged wilderness areas of Grand Canyon, Zion, and Bryce have played an important role in the recovery of peregrine falcons in the Southwest. Few would dispute the fact that peregrines (*Falco peregrinus*) are the most striking raptors that visitors may see.

A male peregrine can be identified by its intense features: dark gray head feathers that resemble a helmet; pointed "falcon" wings and tail; and occasionally dark streaks on its white chest. Females are a darker brown on top and bottom. Both males and females are about the size of ravens but deadly accurate in hunting prey—almost exclusively other birds—thanks to exceptional vision. A biologist floating the Colorado River in Grand Canyon witnessed a peregrine soaring 3,200 feet overhead suddenly dive bomb and snatch a violet-green swallow as it streaked just above the water.

The peregrine's beauty is most apparent when it is in flight. The bird glides at impressive speeds, and its acute eyesight makes it a very effective hunter of waterfowl and other birds. In urban areas like Phoenix and Salt Lake City, wildlife watchers have been surprised at the sight of reintroduced peregrines passing between skyscrapers in pursuit of pigeons. But the human imagination is most stimulated when peregrines are viewed in their native habitat.

According to ornithologists, the remote rock outcroppings of all three parks are excellent nesting places for peregrines. And indeed the peregrine population that resides in the parks is one reason scientists are optimistic about the bird's recovery from declines related to the pesticide DDT. The peregrine is afforded protection under the federal Endangered Species Act.

Another member of the family *Falconidae* that visitors are likely to see in all three parks is the American kestrel (*Falco sparverius*) which is known more commonly as the sparrowhawk. The parks are home to both resident and migrant kestrels, which are observed routinely in all habitats from high alpine terrain to lower deserts. These elegantly colored birds of prey are about the size of a jay and marked with a rufous (brownish-red) back that has dark streaks. It will hover in the air for minutes at a stretch before dropping to catch its prey of small birds.

Where To Find Peregrine Falcons

It is essential that humans leave these birds of prey alone, particularly during the nesting season. Park officials are discreet about publicly identifying the exact locations of peregrine nests because of concerns about disturbance and poaching. Floaters, however, continue to see peregrines in the Grand Canyon and hikers have seen them in the amphitheater area of Bryce Canyon.

WILD TURKEY

Although in some ways it seems incongruous to think of wild turkeys inhabiting what are primarily desert parks, these ostentatious birds are one of the many surprises that wildlife watchers will discover. The wild turkey (*Meleagris gallopavo*) is the largest bird species in the parks.

The turkey has been introduced to several areas of the lower 48 states and Canada, but it was native to Arizona and historically probably had at least a limited presence in the vicinity of Grand Canyon. Efforts by wildlife officials to transplant turkeys have expanded their range to now include portions of Utah around Zion and Bryce.

Toms flaunt their plumage while strutting and some have compared the display of male turkeys to that of the peacock. Indeed, the colors and plumage of a male is arresting. During the strut, the male will extend his tail like a fan and fluff up the feathers on his body. A distinctive focal point is the head, which on a male is bald with bluish coloration on the crown and back of the neck; red festooned with wattles in the area of the throat. In the sunlight, the brown feathers possess a penetrating—almost iridescent—quality and a feathered beard hangs from the breast. Notice, too, the brown-white striped wings. A full-grown male may stand four feet high at its head.

Females are one fourth smaller than the toms and less colorful. They are quite attentive to the brood and vocal if intruders approach. While females cluck, males gobble. At several forest locations it is possible to see turkey flocks. Despite their jumbo appearance, they are excellent flyers and will take off to flee coyotes, bobcats, mountain lions, and even birds of prey which are their primary predators.

The turkey belongs to the family *Phasianidae*, which includes pheasants, grouse, partridges and quail. In short, this grouping refers to what hunters call upland game birds but in national parks, of course, hunting is not allowed, explaining why these turkeys exhibit little fear of humans.

Where To Find Wild Turkeys

They can be observed in coniferous forest and pinyon-juniper-oak areas.

GREAT HORNED OWL

The great horned owl (*Bubo virginianus*) is one of the largest owls found in North America and it is an important part of the ecosystem in all three parks. A furtive nighttime flyer, the great horned is not viewed as easily as other birds of prey because it uses the cloak of darkness to its advantage yet it does hunt on the margins of daylight which makes it crepuscular instead of diurnal or nocturnal. Some refer to it as the "Cat owl," but upon hearing the great horned hoot there is no mistaking this bird which has all the features of a classic owl.

Owls have long stalked prey in the region. The oldest known record of an owl, that of a fossil dating back 60 million years, was found on the Colorado Plateau.

The great horned is so-named because of its ear tufts rising above the eyes which look like "horns." Most of its plumage has a barred, almost striped appearance at close inspection. The prime features for identification are the owls' enormous size (between 18 and 25 inches long); its vocalizations, which really do echo with a soft "hoo-hooo"; the ear tufts; and the circular feather pattern around the yellow eyes. The face has a small beak that is situated between white-gray feathers that look like a mustache and below a white throat "bib."

Of course, excellent hearing and eyesight that can utilize the dimmest of light enables the owl to navigate at the forest edge and hunt reptiles, mice, and other rodents. Retractable talons enable it to easily pluck its prey while still in flight. The great horned is the most common owl native to the parks and a stable population breeds here. It will build its nest in the hollow of a tree and hatch its young during the spring. It hunts in all habitats except open water. Owls become most active when other birds of prey—eagles, hawks, and falcons—retire for the night.

The great horned is fairly ubiquitous in the Americas, found from the southern tundra to lower South America. It lives year-round in the national parks. Another owl, smaller than the great horned, also resides and breeds in the parks. The Flammulated owl (*Otus Flammeolus*) is about half the size of the great horned and appears in both a gray and a rust plummage on top with a whitish-gray belly that is streaked in brown or dark bars. This owl, in contrast to the great horned, has dark eyes.

Where To Find Great Horned Owls

Bryce Canyon: Occasionally, they can be seen at the forest edge near the Lodge shortly after the sun sets. A better place is to stake out any of the amphitheater overlooks. Flammulated owls are modestly abundant in the park's Ponderosa pine forest. Occasionally, park naturalists will supervise nighttime nature walks and call to them.

Grand Canyon: At the North Rim, just around dusk, sit quietly at the Point Imperial lookout as the great horned emerges from the forest to hunt mice racing along the rim.

COMMON RAVEN

One of the truly outstanding but little-known wildlife watching opportunities in the national parks involves the spring congregation of common ravens at Bryce Canyon. As many as 4,000 of them assemble at the treetops in mass, creating a raucas convention. During late autumn, winter, and early spring the park is a staging area for the birds before they return to their normal nesting areas around the Southwest.

The raven (*Corvus corax*) is the largest member of the crow family and frequently sighted in the national parks where it is common. You see them at developed areas and in the wilderness. They are opportunists and will feed upon garbage the same as they will the carcass of a wild animal.

Although several members of the crow family are represented in the parks, the raven has all of what we might consider classic crow markings. Big, coal-black, brazen, and one fourth larger than the American crow, the raven will announce its presence with a boisterous "kraaak-krah" that is distinct from the crow's "kaw." Ravens also are distinct from the crow in that their black beaks are longer than a crow's and the feathers around their head and throat are scruffy and appear disheveled.

Ravens may be seen soaring like raptors, intermittently gliding and flapping. It is against park regulations to feed ravens. Instead, let them pursue their normal staples, like carrion, bird eggs and young, berries, and insects.

Where To Find Common Ravens

Grand Canyon: During the summer, ravens will mass in open meadows along the road to the North Rim, hopping along the ground as they forage for grasshoppers. It is a delightful behavior to watch.

Zion: Ravens can be seen virtually anywhere in the park but they frequently can be viewed along the main park road as it parallels the Virgin River.

Bryce Canyon: Thousands of ravens mass here in the late autumn, winter, and early spring. The best places for observing them are the overlooks, particularly Sunset Point in the main amphitheater.

GAMBEL'S QUAIL

These fast-flying upland birds, which are hunted outside Grand Canyon and Zion parks, are beautifully ornamented. The Gambel's quail (*Callipepla gambelii*) is similar to the better known California quail and, in fact, these birds are able to survive in the Southwest deserts where California Quail cannot.

The male Gambel's head looks as though it is wrapped by a purple-red turban with a small gray feather plume rising above it. Notice, too, on males the white streaks—one streaks across its

forehead and another begins at the eye and slants down toward the neck. The face and throat are black. Females are a duller brown and gray but also have the feather plume. On the breast, the male Gambel's sports a black patch that is surrounded by the tan-yellow belly and also a flare of the same purple-red which appears on the head.

These quail also are fairly large—the size of a small chicken—standing nearly a foot off the ground. Breeding in Grand Canyon and Zion, they reside here year-round and are common in creosotebush, blackbrush, sage, and grasslands. They group up in coveys, and explode into flight from their hiding places on the ground. Their chief predators are coyotes, bobcats, foxes, and birds of prey. They are found in desert areas below 4,500 feet.

Where To Find Gambel's Quail

Hikers are likely to flush the Gambel's quail as they walk through the desert.

119

Black-chinned Hummingbird

HUMMINGBIRD

You may, at first, mistake the black-chinned hummingbird (*Archilochus alexandri*) for a big bumble bee as it whirs through a park campground. But don't despair, these delightful neo-tropical birds are only there to collect nectar from plants or the sugar-water in feeders often hung from recreational vehicles.

This hummer has come a long way to get to the parks from climates in Central and South America. Male black-chins appear, on the surface, to resemble many of the other green-plumed hummingbirds but what sets them apart, of course, are their black chins. By following their beaks in toward their eyes, notice the black throat and white collar. Between the black bar and the white patch you may also see a patch of iridescent violet. Females do not have the black throat or the violet but the rest of their markings are similar to a male's—green feathers on top with a whitishgreen breast.

120

Despite these markings, it still might be difficult differentiating the black-chinned from its close relative, Costa's hummingbird (*Calypte costae*) which also is seasonally abundant and breeds in the parks. The male Costa's has a throat patch that is far more pronounced in its violet color than the black-chinned, and females of both species appear similar except that the female Costa's has a faint red patch on its throat. If you have any doubts, examine the habitat. Costa's hummingbirds prefer drier conditions like those found in country rich with creosote bush and blackbrush, while the black-chinned are found in grasslands and forested areas. Females of both species have white tips on their tails.

A third species of common hummer is the broad-tailed hummingbird (*Selasphorus platycercus*). Broad-tails breed in the parks, though visitors will see far greater numbers in the spring and autumn. Males of this species have a rose-red throat and a broad, continuous tail. The easiest way to distinguish female broad-tails from black-chins and Costa's is to note their size (they usually are larger) and their light brown bellies tinged with reddish-brown (rufous) coloring. They too, have white tips on their tails, just like black-chins and Costa's.

It is against park regulations to artificially feed any wildlife, though many park visitors hang out sugar-water feeders in the campgrounds and attract all three species. Some say it has led to artificially high numbers of black-chins and Costa's existing in the parks. When they are not sipping sugar water at the artificial feeders there is a wealth of blooming wildflowers to satiate them.

Where To Find Hummingbirds

In Grand Canyon, Zion and Bryce, they are numerous in campgrounds, and along river corridors where there is an abundance of wildflowers in the spring and summer.

SWIFT AND SWALLOW

At night, with the summer sun setting across the Bryce Canyon amphitheater and the Grand Canyon rim and the red slickrock canyons in Zion, you will see birds skittering through the vermillion sky alongside bats feasting on insects drawn into the cooling air. Those small birds are white-throated swifts (*Aeronautes saxatalis*) and violet-green swallows (*Tachycineta thalassina*) fluttering their wings and performing acrobatics. It is nature's way of controlling pesky bugs.

In the twilight it might be difficult to tell the two species apart because they are remarkably similar in appearance and behavior. Both build nests beneath rocky overhangs and buildings and they are summer residents only, departing the parks in the autumn for southern or coastal sanctuaries. They are members of two different families, swifts from the *Apodidae* clan and swallows from the *Hurundinidae* family.

With binoculars, you will discover that the white-throated swift has vastly different markings from the violet-green swallow. The swift has black and white markings, most notably a broad patch of white beneath its chin that runs down the middle of its belly as well as white strips along the back of the wings and on the sides near the tail. When it calls, its banter carries well through the chasms of air it explores. Swifts meticulously construct nests of feathers, leaves, grasses, twigs, and mud by gluing them together with saliva. On a preferred shear cliff wall with cover from the elements, many swifts may erect nests. They fly with amazing agility and can dive at high speeds into a swarm of edible insects.

Violet-green swallows, like their swallow brethren, seem as if they were naturally engineered for tricky flight. They are noted for their green heads and backs that have one strip of purple behind the neck and another just above the tail. Their wings are dark but their entire underside is white to the eye and beak.

Flying at speeds approaching 100 miles per hour, you will notice that swifts emit a shrill, high-pitched patter and swallows four or five chirps.

Swift

Both species of birds breed in the park and in addition to being summer residents they pass through the parks in autumn and spring on their way to and from other breeding and wintering areas.

Where To Find Swifts and Swallows

They are seen in open canyons and along rivers in all three parks.

CLARK'S NUTCRACKER

The Clark's nutcracker (*Nucifraga columbiana*) is a bird that shows no fear of humans, and is well suited as a member of the crow clan. These nutcrackers are abundant in Ponderosa pine and fir forests which occur at elevations of 7,500 feet and higher. If it were black, the nutcracker would indeed be mistaken for a crow but its markings allow it to subtlely appear in the trees without alarming those watching it.

Their gray bodies are accented by black on the wings and tail, with a splash of white on the wingtips and the outer tail feathers. The head is set off by black eyes and a long, pointed, dark-gray bill. And yes, they really do eat pine nuts and other seeds, as well as berries and animal carcasses.

Clark's nutcrackers take their name from Capt. William Clark, a co-leader of the Lewis and Clark Expedition, which charted a route from St. Louis to the Pacific Ocean between 1804 and 1806. Like other talkative members of the crow family, they emit a "kraa." Although they seem comfortable around picnic areas, resist the temptation to feed them, for habituation to human handouts compromises their ability to forage for wild foods and ultimately jeopardizes their survival.

In their quest to harvest seeds, Clark's nutcrackers have inadvertently become silviculturists, or cultivators of forest trees. After extracting conifer nuts from the cone, they bury the nuts in the ground for later consumption. But they fail to retrieve all of the seeds and, as a result, new seedlings sprout. Clark's nutcrackers breed in the parks and live here year-round.

Where To Find Clark's Nutcrackers

Grand Canyon: They are abundant along both the South and North Rims.

Zion: They are visible along the Virgin River.

Bryce Canyon: They can be seen along the turnouts overlooking the amphitheater.

GALLERY

SKUNK

The white back stripe, poised black body, and raised tail, can only indicate one thing shortly before the animal strikes olfactory dread into the face of its agitator: Don't mess around with skunks. While the striped skunk (*Mephitis mephitis*) is far more common in the desert Southwest, the Western spotted skunk (*Spilogale gracilis*) also is present. Both species are capable of discharging the skunk's trademark, powerful spray, which originates in glands near the animal's posterior but it is not given gratuitously, rather only to those who provoke the encounter. Skunks, which can weigh between 5 and 15 pounds, are far more common in developed areas around the perimeter of parks than at higher-elevation sights inside of them. Keeping a clean camp in skunk country is important. One incentive is the fact that skunks still are a prime carrier of rabies in the lower 48 states.

GRAY FOX

The most astonishing characteristic of gray foxes, unknown to most people, is the fact that these wild dogs can climb trees, the only canid in North America capable of such a feat. While the red fox is certainly more ubiquitous across the lower 48 states, the gray fox endures in the hardscrabble hill and forest country of all three national parks where land unbroken by significant development is more to its liking. Sightings of gray fox (*Urocyon cinereoargenteus*) are infrequent in the parks but part of this may be due to the greater presence of coyotes. Like all foxes, the gray is extremely wary around humans and prefers to make its den, which is used all winter long, in obvious places such as inside caves, rock structures, even inside hollow standing trees.

The gray fox's tree-climbing skills give it added versatility in foraging. When not scrounging for rodents, berries or other natural fruits on the ground, it may turn its attention skyward and feast upon the contents of bird nests. When finished, it will sling its body over the limb of a tree and nap without fear of being attacked by coyotes or bobcats on the ground.

Inside the national parks, where hunting is not permitted, the gray fox is more active during the daylight hours though it remains primarily a nocturnal creature that will roam dozens of miles in a single night.

RACCOON

Common to most of the lower 48 states, the raccoon (*Procyon lotor*) has become synony- mous with roadside camping because these nighttime bandits are notorious for raiding caches of human food. Still, while raccoons exist within the vicinity of the three parks, it is their cousin, the ringtail, which is far more common. Raccoons can be identified by their classic dark "mask" and bushy striped tail. In addition, their tracks bear a striking resemblance to a human's foot—only with claw marks.

DESERT COTTONTAIL

If you see a rabbit in any of the three parks, it is probably a desert cottontail (*Sylvilagus audubonii*), which is common in sagebrush, grassland, and scrub- pine forests. Such habi- tat offers the desert cottontail not only sources of food but cover in which to evade predators. This animal can be identified by the mottled brown fur on its back, white belly, tan legs and classic white "cotton" tail. Foremost, when you see a desert cottontail scampering about you will see the elongated ears that perk as it scavenges for grasses.

A unique feature of desert cottontails is the fact that they, like most rabbits and hares, are coprophages, which means they consume their own fecal droppings as a way of recycling the undigested nutrients. In a desert environment, where food can be scarce, it makes the search for food less brutal. Two other less common rabbits found in the same area are the gray-white black-tailed jack rabbit (*Lepus californicus*) and the grayish-brown Nuttall's cottontail (*Sylvilagus nuttallii*) also called the mountain cottontail. The primary predators of all three species are coyotes, bobcats, and birds of prey. As they flee coyotes and other predators, black-tailed jack rabbits will run in a zig-zag pattern to evade their pursuers. They are most visible in the evening hours just before sunset. Desert cottontails can be seen in campgrounds and around visitor centers as well as along backcountry trails.

YELLOW-BELLIED MARMOT

The yellow-bellied marmot (*Marmota fla-viventris*) is found at middle to upper elevations in the parks and occupy similar areas as pikas. As the name implies, the yellow-bellied marmot has a belly covered with yellowish fur, darker brownish-yellow fur on its back, a stubby, bush tail of the same color, and whitish-yellow markings on the face and chin. A binocular view will reveal the animal's resemblance to the groundhog. They prefer to set up their burrow in jumbles of boulders which provide cover and a means to evade predators, including coyotes, bobcats, and hawks. When threatened, yellow-bellieds retreat to a safe hiding place and begin emitting whistling sounds which is why some have called them "whistle pigs." The viewing season for yellow-bellieds is short. Like ground squirrels, yellow-bellieds hibernate and will disappear into dens by mid September only to reemerge half a year later.

GOLDEN-MANTLED GROUND SQUIRREL

Many people wonder why the golden-mantled ground squirrel (*Spermophilus lateralis*) is called "king of the beasts" at many park locations, but when you visit developed areas you'll understand why. These chipmunk-like squirrels are abundant throughout all three parks though unfortunately feeding of the animals by park visitors has rendered them to be beggars.

Colored with orange fur and a flag of black to white stripes on their back, golden-mantles are quite active in the spring and summer months as they try to build their supplies of body fat before the deep sleep of hibernation that occurs during the winter. Vegetarians, golden-mantled squirrels eat grasses, insects, berries, and nuts, and often are seen collecting food in their cheek pouches. True to their name, these rodents, though they are capable of climbing trees and buildings, erect their nests in underground dens.

Ground squirrels, particularly those that have been fed human snacks, appear to be exceptionally large chipmunks. Trying to tell the difference between ground squirrels and chipmunks can be confusing particularly if you're trying to do it based upon the black and white stripes that flank their backs. An easier way to distinguish them is to look at their facial markings. If the animal has streaks of white and black running across its cheeks, it is likely to be the least chipmunk (*Tamias minimus*), Uinta chipmunk (*Tamias umbrinus*) or the cliff chipmunk (*Tamias dorsalis*). If no streaks appear, it's the golden-mantled ground squirrel. Golden mantles also have tails that are less fluffy than a chipmunk's. Golden mantles hibernate in winter; chipmunks do not and rely upon foods they have stored in their burrows.

In Zion and Grand Canyon at lower elevations, one of the most common chipmunk-like species is the White-tailed Antelope squirrel (*Ammospermophilus leucurus*).

Golden mantles and their cousin, the chipmunk, are ubiquitous in both Bryce and Grand Canyon. Prime viewing areas are the overlooks along the amphitheater and near the lodge in Bryce Canyon, and at cabin and campground areas of both the North and South Rims of the Grand Canyon. Golden mantles are not common in Zion National Park.

JAYS

The seventh member of the crow family mentioned in this book and found in all three parks are the jays—the Steller's, the Pinyon, and the Scrub. All three are most prevalent in the pinyon-juniper-oak forests found at higher elevations, and it is hard to miss them. The most obvious of them is the Steller's jay (*Cyanocitta stelleri*). Imagine a blue jay flaunting a dark mohawk haircut. That's the Steller's. It also has deep blue wings with bars running across them and lighter, iridescent blue across its belly and tail. Its beak is long and pointed. The Pinyon jay (*Gymnohinus cyanocephalus*) looks

Steller's Jay

somewhat similar to the Steller's except that it doesn't have the feathered head crest nor the dark coloration on the head. It is more of a sky-slate blue and has a short tail. The Scrub jay (*Aphelocoma coerulescens*) can be identified by its long blue tail, and a body that has a white throat area and a brownish back. Omnivores all, this trio nests in conifers and will eat insects, berries, seeds, and young birds. They frequently announce their presence with a harsh "kaw" or "kreh" and they will mimic the calls of other birds. Steller's jays are the biggest of the three, reaching standing heights of just over a foot, followed by Scrub jays which are only slightly smaller, and Pinyon jays slightly smaller still. They are common to forested campgrounds in all three parks.

TURKEY VULTURE

The circling of turkey vultures (*Cathartes aura*) high in the sky is supposed to tell us that something has died. It's a cliche, yes, but these rather unhandsome scavengers—which really do resemble wild turkeys—are fixtures in the Southwest. Their presence reminds us that life can be tough in the desert and that only those animals that take advantage of all circumstances will survive. Some claim that vultures can smell rotting flesh from half a mile in the air.

Besides the black wing spans that can stretch to nearly six feet across and form a V pattern, you'll probably notice the turkey vulture's red naked head on adult birds (immature birds have pale black heads). Turkey vultures assemble in bands where carrion is available. The birds will aggressively guard their find against other birds and have been known to drive mammalian scavengers off carcasses as well. Look for them in the sky. Underneath, their wings are colored by black underwings and slate gray secondaries and primaries. When walking, a long tail and red talons are present. They are seen in all three parks and are known to breed in Zion. It is impossible to predict where a turkey vulture may be seen but they are especially prevalent in the winter and spring, feeding on winter-killed animals.

BLACK-BILLED MAGPIE

Black-billed mag-pies (*Pica pica*) may be the most colorfully ostentatious birds in the park even though their colors are pre-dominately black and white. Members of the crow family, they are bold scavengers whose black and white pattern on their wings attracts attention.

Visitors will see magpies in campgrounds and developed areas of the parks. Although they commonly eat road-killed animals, car-casses, natural fruits, grasshoppers, and other insects, magpies will not hesitate to steal human food left behind on a picnic table. Unfortunately, humans who violate the Park Service policy against feeding wildlife have created a group of beggars in magpies.

Few wildlife watchers will forget the decorated markings of a black-billed magpie. The bird's scientific name means black and white, and it describes the black-billed bird perfectly. It has pen-etrating black plumage that covers the head and runs the length of the back across a long greenish-black, almost glowing tail. Part of its underside and front scapular, however, is bright white. Magpies are year-round residents of the parks.

LONG-TAILED WEASEL

Neurotic, curious, and pound-for-pound a ferocious predator, weasels move so subtly through the landscape that they are seldom noticed. But if you are patient and wait quietly beside a stream particularly in the early morning hours, you may see one of the most proficient hunters at work. The long-tailed weasel (*Mustela frenata*) is mink like in its appearance. At maturity, an adult weighs less than eight ounces, yet it takes on prey twice its size, including birds and rodents. Although it is capable of climbing trees it spends most of its time on the ground and lives in the abandoned burrows of other animals. A typical home range for a longtail is between 30 and 40 acres. In northern latitudes, the longtail's coat changes to white to match the snowcover. Longtails are found at all elevations—in meadows and forests, near campgrounds, and in the remotest wilderness outpost.

ROADRUNNER

BEEP-BEEP. Despite the familiarity of the popular cartoon character, most people really know very little about greater roadrunners (*Geococcyx californianus*) yet their interest is high. Roadrunners are observed in Grand Canyon and Zion every year but not in sufficient enough numbers to make them common. Rather, sightings occur irregularly but with great delight. The profile of a roadrunner is unmistakable primarily because everything on its body seems so long— the brown tail that has white edges at the end; its gangly legs that leave tracks showing two toes forward; and its long beak that sticks out from a head that bears a shaggy crest. The color of this cuckoo is streaked in brown and tan. The area directly behind its eyes has a colorful, reddish streak. The roadrunner emits a series of "koos" when it is alarmed. A species adapted to the desert, it hunts for lizards, caterpillars, seeds, and berries. And yes, it really does flee by running on the ground from birds of prey and coyotes, which are its chief enemy. A bird that is more abundant in the Grand Canyon than the roadrunner and part of the same family is the Groove-billed Ani (*Crotophaga sulcirostris*) which has dark-black plumage with a black bill that looks like that of a puffin. It also has a long, black, rounded, parrot-like tail. The roadrunner is found year-round in most low desert terrain and the Ani is abundant throughout the canyon area.

HAIRY WOODPECKER

One of about half a dozen woodpeckers found in the parks, the hairy woodpecker (*Picoides villosus*) is the most common and occupies primarily the pinyon and Ponderosa pine forests where it bores holes in trees to create cavity nests and to feed on insects which infest the wood. The hairy is most noted for its black and white feather patterns across its body and the obvious red patch on the top of its head. It has black, sometimes a black and white checkered pattern, on its wings, a white underbelly, and a long dark bill. It is similar in its appearance to the downy woodpecker which is rare in the regions of the parks. Hairy woodpeckers can be seen on both rims of the Grand Canyon, in Zion and throughout Bryce.

BLUE GROUSE

A typical resident of brushy ridgelines that rise above successional forest is the blue grouse (*Dendragapus obscurus*). It is occasionally spotted along the roadside and in higher elevations, but it more often surprises back-country hikers who inadvertently startle it. This bird, regarded as a game species outside the park, is a non-migratory relative that belongs to the same family as the wild turkey. Blue grouse forage on grasshoppers, juniper berries, and other plants during the warm summer but switch to conifer needles as a winter staple. Contrary to its name, the male grouse is not truly blue, but a faint, bluish gray; the male flaunts an orange-gray comb near its eyes and a purple pouch that becomes visible during the spring mating dance. Hens are brown. The courtship jig is conducted by the male, which tries to gain the attention of hens by filling and deflating its neck pouch, emitting what some ornithologists call "booms" and "hoots." The dance often is performed on a log. The blue grouse moves to higher elevations in winter, burrowing in snowpack as insulation against the cold. Blue grouse are seen at the higher elevations in Zion and the southern end of Bryce as well as the rim areas of Grand Canyon.

SO YOU'D LIKE TO KNOW MORE?

Here's a list of sources for more information about wildlife watching in the parks.

Grand Canyon National Park, c/o Superintendent, P.O. Box 129, Grand Canyon, AZ 86023

Zion National Park, c/o Superintendent, Springdale, UT 84767

Bryce Canyon National Park, c/o Superintendent, Bryce Canyon, UT 84717-1099

Watchable Wildlife

To learn more about Watchable Wildlife Programs in national parks near you, write to: Defenders of Wildlife, 1244 19th St NW, Washington, DC 20036 or The National Park Service, c/o Wildlife and Vegetation Division, P.O. Box 37127, Washington, D.C. 20013.

Grand Canyon Natural History Association

For the average visitor, the Grand Canyon is so vast that it's hard to know where to begin. The Grand Canyon Natural History Association has dedicated itself to protecting park resources by promoting better understanding of Grand Canyon's cultural and natural history. A membership in this non-profit group goes a long way not only toward staying informed about things to do in the park but members enjoy a discount on books, access to slide shows, nature walks, and periodic information about special events happening in the park. For more information about how you can become a park steward, write: Grand Canyon Natural History Association, P.O. Box 399, Grand Canyon, AZ 86023.

Grand Canyon Field Institute

Its unofficial name is "the University of the Grand Canyon," but one thing is certain, nothing beats the Grand Canyon Field Institute in providing opportunities to gain an intimate and educational glimpse into one of the true natural wonders of the world. A variety of classes are offered ranging from wilderness medicine and outdoor photography to seminars on Hopi Indian culture and the ecology of birds. An outgrowth of the Grand Canyon Natural History Association, the classes are open to students of all ages. For a catalog and membership information, write: Grand Canyon Field Institute, P.O. Box 399, Grand Canyon, AZ 86023.

Zion Natural History Association

This group is considered one of the best nature education organizations in the United States and a contribution to ZNHA is an investment in the future of Zion's flora and fauna. Member wildlife watchers receive information about special nature walks and slide shows, and they receive a discount on books, maps, videos, and other merchandise. For membership information, write: Zion Natural History Association, Zion National Park, Springdale, UT 84767.

Bryce Canyon Natural History Association

Each year this group offers a line of books and other educational materials. The proceeds from these publications help fund interpretive programs and research in the park so that wildland managers can make better decisions. Note: There are no memberships. For more information, write: Bryce Canyon Natural History Association, Bryce Canyon, UT 84717.

SELECTED READING LIST

America's Neighborhood Bats by Merlin D. Tuttle

Animal Tracks by Olaus J. Murie (Peterson Field Guide)

Audubon Society Field Guide to North American Mammals
by John O. Whitaker, Jr.

Audubon Society Field Guide to North American Birds
by Miklos Udvardy

Birds of Prey on the Colorado Plateau
by Museum of Northern Arizona

Grand Canyon National Park: A Natural History
by Jeremy Schmidt

Mammals by Peter Alden (Peterson Field Guide)

National Geographic's Guide to the National Parks

Poisonous Dwellers of the Desert by Natt N. Dodge

Venomous Animals & Poisonous Plants by Steven Foster and
Roger Caras (Peterson Field Guide)

Western Birds by Roger Tory Peterson

Western Reptiles and Amphibians by R.C. Stebbing
(Peterson Field Guide)